CROWN HIM LORD OF ALL

ESSAYS ON THE LIFE AND WITNESS OF THE FREE CHURCH OF SCOTLAND

Clement Graham

CROWN HIM LORD OF ALL

ESSAYS ON THE LIFE AND WITNESS OF THE FREE CHURCH OF SCOTLAND

Clement Graham

THE KNOX PRESS (EDINBURGH)

THE KNOX PRESS (EDINBURGH)
15 North Bank Street, Edinburgh EH1 2LS

First published 1993
ISBN 0 904422 41 0

Typeset by BP Integraphics Ltd, Bath, Avon
and printed by The Bath Press

Contents

The Contributors

MAURICE GRANT, a civil servant, and an elder in St. Columba's Free Church, Edinburgh. Deeply interested in Church history he has already written a book on the Covenanter Donald Cargill, entitled *No King but Christ.*

DAVID A. ROBERTSON, one of the younger ministers of the Free Church. Until recently he was minister at Brora and has now taken up a new and challenging work in the city of Dundee centred on St. Peter's, the church associated with R.M. McCheyne.

HECTOR CAMERON, minister in places as diverse as London and Wick. Widely appreciated as a Christian apologist with a flair for presenting truth in vivid idiom.

A.P.W. FRASER, minister at Elgin and for many years assistant clerk of Assembly. Has comprehensive knowledge of music and writes with authority on the songs of the Church.

W.D. GRAHAM, minister in Fife and Edinburgh before taking up work as missionary in Southern Africa, presently Principal of Dumisani Bible School which specialises in correspondence courses of eduction both for candidates for the ministry and people anxious to develop knowledge of what the Bible teaches.

RONALD MACKENZIE, minister at Glenelg and formerly at Coigach, both parishes in the North West of Scotland. Clerk of the Presbytery of Lochcarron.

WILLIAM M. MACKAY has been involved in Christian education all his working life. He was Headmaster of the Colegio San Andrés in Lima, Peru and is now Headmaster of a College in Melbourne, Australia.

CLEMENT GRAHAM, after a ministry in Tain, Ross-shire, taught in the Free Church College, Edinburgh. He is presently Principal Clerk of the General Assembly.

Introduction

On 18 May 1843 there took place an event which stirred the populace of Scotland as few events before or since have done. This was the separation from the Church of Scotland of a significant proportion of its ministers, elders and people to form the Free Church of Scotland. To be sure, it had not been the intention of the leaders of the separated movement to disrupt the Church. They would have been delighted if the whole Church had joined with them in the new movement and so retained the integrity of the Church of Scotland. What they felt compelled to break was the bond between Church and State.

Church and State they viewed as institutes of God and as such mandated to respect each other's sphere of responsibility and to be helpful to one another. The State's help to the Church should be in procuring civil liberty for people to meet for worship, and to aid the Church financially and materially to carry on its work to promote the ends of godliness. In no way should the provision of such help be regarded as implying a right on the part of the State to interfere in the spiritual administration of the Church. The Church is subject to Christ as its sole Head and His Word is its authoritative rule of life. The calling and settling of ministers in congregations is therefore to be regulated by the Church in its understanding and application of Scripture. The State has no right to interfere in this area. But in the years prior to 1843 the State did interfere – lending its authority to the intrusion of unwanted ministers into congregations and interdicting Presbyteries from inducting ministers duly called by congregations and approved by the Church.

What was at stake was the spiritual independence of the Church and as this independence was a gift of the Lord Himself and subject always, and, ultimately only, to His sovereignty, its annulment was seen as defiance of the 'Crown Rights of Jesus'. Just as the Covenanters in earlier days had contended 'for Christ's Crown and

Covenant' so the leaders of the Free Church felt duty bound to proclaim the Crown Rights of Jesus in His Church. If the cost of State help was to be the denial of these rights then the help of the State would have to be declined and the Church would go it alone. And so was born the Church of Scotland Free – still persuaded that a good and helpful relationship with the State should be desired but sadly admitting that for that time this relationship was impossible. In the oft-quoted words of Dr. Thomas Chalmers 'We quit a vitiated Establishment but we would rejoice in returning to a pure one'.

That was 150 years ago and the Church formed then still continues, maintaining the commitment to Biblical truth that was articulated at the time of the Reformation. The following chapters give some account of the history and contemporary activities of the Church. The history has not been untroubled and the present situation is not without its full share of difficulties, not least difficulties connected with the material support of the Church's ventures. But the Church still looks to its sole King and Head and prosecutes its various enterprises in reliance upon His grace, provision and guidance – still jealous of the Crown Rights of Jesus.

1

The Heirs of the Disruption in Crisis and Recovery 1893–1920

MAURICE GRANT

THE EBB TIDE

The Disruption of 1843 reaffirmed two great principles of the Scottish Reformation. One – the principle of spiritual independence, or the right of the Church to manage her own affairs – was understandably given greater prominence. But the other – the duty of the State to support the Church, or the 'establishment principle' as it was known – was no less vigorously asserted by the Disruption Fathers. At a time when they were quitting the Establishment, it might perhaps have been expected that Thomas Chalmers and his followers would have thought somewhat less kindly of the establishment principle. But this was by no means the case. While the existing Establishment had failed them, they saw no reason on that account to abandon the establishment principle. 'Though we quit the Establishment', declared Chalmers, 'we go out on the establishment principle; we quit a vitiated Establishment, but would rejoice in returning to a pure one' (Moderatorial Address, 1843). That commitment, though it remained unfulfilled, was to assume great significance for the Free Church at later stages of her history.

The Disruption was not merely an ecclesiastical event of the first importance; it was also a great movement of the people. The work of the Disruption Church was carried along on a tide of popular enthusiasm. To that, at the human level, the Church owed much of its early success. That success was mirrored in a remarkable range of practical achievements. New churches and manses were built, theological colleges opened, an extensive educational system developed, and thriving missions opened overseas. To any dispassionate onlooker, it must have seemed that the Free Church was enjoying in a very singular manner the blessing of God. And, across large areas of her work, that was undoubtedly true.

But the lessons of Scripture and history show that material prosperity can often be a snare to the Church of God. So, alas, it was to prove for the Free Church. As memories of the Disruption faded, and the tide of spiritual fervour began to wane, there developed a sense of self-satisfaction with the gains achieved. The successes of the past, and the prospects for the future, began to be seen increasingly in man-centred, rather than God-centred terms. In process of time, this tendency was to prove disastrous for the Free Church. Some, indeed, had the foresight to detect the danger at an early stage. It was the view of the noted Rev. Archibald Cook of Daviot, not long after the Disruption, that 'the Lord would not honour the Free Church, because they had too much pride in what they did'.

The new tendency began to manifest itself in a number of ways. Its first and most obvious expression was in a desire for union with other churches. The Free Church was held in high regard by other non-established Presbyterian churches in Scotland. She had an enviable reputation for getting things done. She was in a strong position to set herself up as a focus for reunion of the various Presbyterian bodies which, over the previous century, had separated from the national church. Such a move would not only reinvigorate Scottish Presbyterianism; it would also create a powerful bastion against the increasing secularisation which was menacing the churches as a whole.

Such was the thinking behind the scheme for Union which was to dominate the counsels of the Church after 1860. It was noteworthy that, unlike the Disruption, the scheme had no strong current of popular support behind it. It was, in its essence, a movement dictated by expediency in which ecclesiastical rather than spiritual issues prevailed. And that, sadly, was to be its hallmark throughout the years that followed.

There was one apparently obvious candidate for union with the Free Church. In 1847, just four years after the Disruption, the Relief and Secession Churches which had separated from the Church of Scotland in the eighteenth century came together to form the United Presbyterian Church. Both Churches were committed to the principle of spiritual independence and the Westminster standards, and they carried these principles with them into their new denomination. But they were also firmly opposed to the establishment principle, and of necessity the new body reflected this view. From the outset, and consistently thereafter, the United Presbyterian Church made it plain that the establishment principle formed no part of its constitution.

However, by the 1860s, this was not seen as a major obstacle to union by the majority in the Free Church. The Disruption was some twenty years in the past, and the emphasis placed on the establishment principle by the Free Church leaders of that time was being quietly lost to sight. In any case, though committed to the establishment principle, the Free Church was no longer part of the Establishment; and it had successfully existed for twenty years without the State connection. In these circumstances, it was tempting to conclude that the establishment principle was little more than an ecclesiastical relic which had little relevance to the contemporary Free Church. Certainly, it should not be allowed to get in the way of union with like-minded Christians who shared the same basic beliefs. And on no account should it allowed to impede the plans for wider Presbyterian union in which the Free Church wished to play a leading part.

Such was the argument deployed by the pro-Union party in the Church; and inevitably it carried a wide appeal. Overtures to the United Presbyterians proved fruitful, and in 1863 a joint Union Committee of the two Churches was set up. This made progress for a time, but soon came up against the obstacle of the establishment principle. The United Presbyterians for their part made it clear that they were not prepared to admit the principle in any form. If therefore any concession was to be made, it was clear that it would have to come from the Free Church; and in 1867 the Free Church Assembly duly obliged when it declared that the difference between the churches on the establishment issue constituted no impediment to union. By this time however a strong minority in the Church had grown alarmed; and an active and vigorous campaign was set afoot to halt the Union movement in its tracks. A major part in this campaign was played by *The Watchword*, a periodical ably edited by Dr James Begg, and by a stream of articles and pamphlets from the pen of Dr Begg's friend and coadjutor, Dr Kennedy of Dingwall. For a time, the threat of another Disruption loomed imminent; but at the last moment wiser counsels prevailed. In face of the continuing opposition the pro-Unionists abandoned their objective and contented themselves with a Mutual Eligibility Act, passed in 1873, which placed United Presbyterian and Free Church ministers on an equal footing as regards calls to vacant charges. There the Union movement ended for the time being; and until it was revived some twenty years later, the pro-Unionists were left to channel their energies in other directions. This they did, with increasing fervour, by mounting a campaign for disestablishment of the national Church, to which end they passed a series of resolutions at successive Assemblies. Though nothing eventually came of this agitation, it evidenced how far the Free Church had now come from espousal of the establishment principle which it had cherished in 1843. And, though they did not recognise it at the time, by adopting this policy the pro-Union party were sowing the seeds of what was to prove their own downfall at a later stage of the Church's history.

Meantime, the Church was setting about to conform itself in doctrine and practice with the spirit of age. A new liberalism was abroad, and the robust Calvinism of earlier days had become distinctly unfashionable. The Moody and Sankey campaign of 1874 gave a distinct impetus to the movement for change and pointed the way towards a more subjective, man-centred presentation of the Gospel. The same event, too, gave added force to a movement, already prevalent in the Church, to bring the Church's mode of worship more into line with modern tastes. This had already found expression in the approval of 1872 of the first Free Church hymn book, and was to culminate eleven years later in the sanctioning of instrumental music in congregational praise. Other time-honoured practices were similarly under threat. The traditional five-day Scottish Communion season with its preparatory and thanksgiving services was increasingly seen as a burdensome relic from the past, and briefer and more frequent Communions became the norm in many areas.

But the main assault of the innovators was directed at the integrity of Scripture itself. This found its fullest expression in the Higher Criticism, an import from Germany, which placed a premium on a rationalistic interpretation of Scripture and discounted the role of supernatural revelation. The new teaching was of course consistent with the humanistic spirit of the age; and its origin in the fount of the German intellect gave it a respectability which it might not otherwise have attained. A system of interpretation espoused by the keenest theological minds in Europe could not fail to be attractive to those in other countries who wished to see themselves as leaders of Biblical thought. Among this class were not a few in the Free Church. From around 1863, when A.B. Davidson was appointed to the New College in Edinburgh, the new teaching began steadily to infiltrate the Church. Davidson himself had drunk deep of German thought, and used his position to influence his students. With the appointment of other teachers of a similar stamp, the new doctrine rapidly gained ground. By the late 1870s, the Higher Criticism had taken a firm hold in the Divinity Halls of the Church. Though its presence was known, and its effects clearly seen, little was done to keep it in check.

The pro-Union majority, for their own ends, were content to tolerate the new teaching in their midst, and the innovators were left largely to their own devices. On occasion, indeed, there was resistance, and the purveyors of the new doctrines were called to account before the General Assembly. The most celebrated such case was that of William Robertson Smith, who in 1870 was appointed to the Chair of Old Testament in the Free Church College at Aberdeen. Robertson Smith had studied under Davidson and subsequently in Germany, and was a leading exponent of the Higher Criticism. In 1875, in an article in the *Encyclopedia Britannica*, he specifically called in question the Mosaic authorship of the Pentateuch. A lengthy process followed in the Church Courts, which led initially to his acquittal by the General Assembly of 1880. But a further, more extreme, article proved his undoing, and the Assembly of 1881 dismissed him from his Chair. By then however the damage had been done. The new teaching continued to permeate the Church, and though complaints were lodged against other professors – notably A.B. Bruce and Marcus Dods, in 1890 – the Assembly refused to take any action other than to deliver mild exhortations to those concerned.

A graphic picture of this dark period of the Church's history was given by Rev. Ewan Macleod in his Moderatorial address to the General Assembly of 1905: 'The leaders in effect said to the retailers of German culture, "If you support our policy we shall tolerate your views to your hearts' content" ... Confessional doctrine came to be seen as unscientific and behind the times. The seed of the new faith was thus sown, and every year's issue of young ministers from the Colleges went to their pulpits with a greatly modified Gospel. The new doctrines began to be publicly preached, and many of the Chairs in the Divinity Halls came to be occupied by men tainted with the new views ... We had annual exhibitions associated with the frittering away of the Church's constitution, doctrine, worship and other matters. We had also painful trials of heretical professors, who persisted in troubling the Church with false doctrine. These proceedings created a wound which was kept open from year to year, and wore out the religious life of the Church' (*The Monthly Record of the Free Church of Scotland*, June 1905). A contemporary comment by C.H. Spurgeon was also sadly to the point: 'The Free Church of Scotland must unhappily be for the moment regarded as rushing to the front with its new theology, which is no theology, but an opposition to the Word of the Lord. That Church in which we all gloried as sound in the faith and full of martyrs' spirit has entrusted the training of its future ministers to professors who hold other doctrines than those of its Confession. This is the most suicidal act a Church could commit' (quoted in J.B. Orr, *Scotch Church Crisis*, 1905, p.21).

THE DECLARATORY ACT CONTROVERSY

The outcome of the Robertson Smith case by no means halted the spread of the Higher Criticism within the Church. On the contrary, it merely aggravated the feelings of those who saw adherence to the Church's confessional standards as a burden too heavy to be borne. A movement was set afoot, connived at if not encouraged by those in leading positions in the Church, to relax the Church's adherence to certain elements of the Westminster Confession of Faith in such a way as to accommodate those who could not in conscience subscribe to them. Though it was not publicly acknowledged at the time, one of the clear objects of this movement was to bring the Free Church into closer harmony with the United Presbyterian Church, which had relaxed its own adherence to the Confession by means of a Declaratory Act passed by its Synod in 1879. Indeed, such was the pervasive influence of the liberal movement that several Presbyterian churches in various parts of the world were taking similar measures; and the Free Church, with its liking for being thought enlightened and forward-looking, certainly did not wish to be left behind.

The clamour for change reached a climax in 1889, when, as the result of a carefully orchestrated campaign, no fewer than 22 overtures seeking review of the Church's attitude to the Confession were presented to the General Assembly (Free Church Assembly Papers, 1889). Despite the fact that a further 12 overtures – all from the Highlands – opposed any change, the Assembly set up a high-powered Committee, with Principal Rainy of New College as Joint Convener, to consider how best to meet the demands. The Committee, after taking two years to complete its work, presented the results of its efforts to the Assembly of 1891. Predictably, its main recommendation was in favour of a Declaratory Act similar to that already in force in the United Presbyterian Church. Its main effect and purpose was to give the liberal element in the Church what they wished; the ability to subscribe the Confession with reservations which, in effect, nullified some of its basic doctrines. The Act, like its United Presbyterian counterpart, set out to modify the Confessional doctrine of the sovereignty of God and to exalt the dignity of man. In its emphasis on man's free will and ability to perform good works, it contained the seeds of Arminian and Pelagian heresies. And, by granting to the Church the right to determine what points in the Confession formed 'the substance of the Reformed Faith', it left the Church without a fixed confessional standard and with no effective defence against the intrusion of heretical teaching or practices.

In face of dissents from a handful of 'constitutionalists' – as those who opposed the Act came to be called – the Act was approved by an overwhelming majority of the Assembly and sent down to Presbyteries for their comments. The months that followed saw considerable agitation in the Church, as opponents of the Act sought to point out its harmful effects and held meetings up and down the country to gain support for their cause. Discontent was particularly strong in the Highlands, reflecting the opposition there had been to the movement for change in the first place, and in not a few places the loyalty of ministers and congregations was placed under serious strain.

At the Assembly of 1892, when the returns from Presbyteries were submitted, it was found that 54 Presbyteries had approved the Act, while only 23 had opposed it. On this basis Principal Rainy felt justified in proposing that the Act be passed into a standing law of the Church; and this was duly approved by 346 votes to 195. Eighteen ministers and seventeen elders – again overwhelmingly from the Highlands – recorded their dissent.

The passing of the Declaratory Act by no means dispelled the opposition to it within the Church. In the Highlands particularly a strong movement was set afoot, with wide popular support, aimed at the Act's repeal. This resulted in the submission of ten overtures from Highland Synods and Presbyteries to the 1893 Assembly. Two Presbyteries and two Kirk Sessions recorded formal protests against the Act in their records; and one Presbytery recorded a protest by a newly-inducted minister that he was taking his induction vows without reference to the Act.

If any hopes had been entertained of the 1893 Assembly, they were soon doomed to disappointment. The Assembly's treatment of the objectors was draconian. The Presbyteries who had recorded protests were ordered to expunge these from their records, and all the overtures craving repeal or merely review of the Act were summarily dismissed. The Assembly had given the clearest possible indication of its intention to abide by the Act and not to tolerate any opposition.

Ever since the movement for change had been initiated in 1889, the constitutionalist ministers had safeguarded their position by dissenting from the findings of the Assembly, and by lodging protests stating that their participation in debates did not commit them in any way to accepting the need for review of the Church's relationship to the Confession. This line had been fully maintained at the Assembly of 1893, when dissents with reasons were lodged against each of the Assembly's findings. However, in the period leading up to the Assembly, and indeed for some time previously, there had been a growing opinion in some parts of the Church that something more than dissent was needed if the conscience of the individual was to be safeguarded from complicity in the pernicious effects of the Act. By the time the 1893 Assembly met, this had crystallised into a movement for separation on the part of some of the Church's most loyal supporters in the Highlands.

The main impetus for the separation movement came from a small but highly articulate body of divinity students, supported by some influential laymen in the north and west. The movement attracted scarcely any support from among the ministers, who, however strongly they felt about the Act, were not on the whole prepared to see it as a necessary cause for separation. One minister however, the Rev. Donald Macfarlane of Raasay, took a different view; and for some time prior to the Assembly of 1893 he had been convinced that, if the Assembly refused to repeal the Act, separation was the only possible response. Mr. Macfarlane had not come to particular prominence in the public debate on the Act, and he was not reckoned to be one of the constitutionalist leaders. He had however been active in a variety of ways at the local level. On 4 May 1892, while minister at Kilmallie, he had convened a meeting of the congregation and others in opposition to the Act, and had sent a strongly-worded petition on their behalf to the General Assembly (Free Church Assembly Papers, 1892). After the Act had been passed, he recorded a protest against it in his Session records; and on his induction to Raasay, on 27 April 1893, he stated before the

Presbytery and congregation that he was answering the questions and subscribing the formula without reference to the Act (*Free Presbyterian Magazine*, September 1923). He had also made public, on at least two occasions, his view that if the Assembly did not repeal the Act, the Church would be faced with a further Disruption (*Inverness Courier*, 9 January 1891; *Northern Chronicle*, 25 January 1893). At the Assembly of 1893, when the overtures craving repeal of the Act were dismissed, Mr. Macfarlane tabled a formal protest in which he claimed his 'sacred and civil rights in accordance with the creed and constitution of the Free Church in the year 1843' and declared that, whatever he might subsequently do, neither his conscience nor his ordination vows allowed him to act under what had now been made law in the Church.

Mr. Macfarlane's action was treated – as it was undoubtedly intended to be – as a repudiation of the Assembly's authority, and on that ground his protest was not received. After leaving the Assembly, Mr. Macfarlane convened a series of public meetings in which he declared his unmistakable intention to separate from the Church. Although only one other minister – the Rev. Donald Macdonald of Shieldaig – declared himself on his side, the movement found support from significant numbers of students and laymen, and from many within the Highland congregations of the Church. On 28 July 1893 the separating body constituted itself as 'The Free Church Presbytery of Scotland' (later to become the Free Presbyterian Church of Scotland), and a formal Deed of Separation was signed at Portree on 14 August.

Mr. Macfarlane had shown his protest in advance to one of the constitutionalist leaders, but he had not revealed his intentions in any formal way. As a result, his action took many of the constitutionalists by surprise. When he followed up his protest with clear steps towards separation, their misgivings grew. It seemed to them that separation would merely damage the constitutionalist cause and fragment what had up to then been a united witness against the Declaratory Act. Their remonstrances however were in vain; and, from a very early stage after his protest, Mr. Macfarlane declared that, for his own part, he regarded the separation as irrevocable. If the Free Church authorities had entertained any doubts on this point, they were soon to be disillusioned. Presbytery deputations sent to reason with the dissenting congregations were met by locked churches and closed doors. The Presbytery of Skye complained to the Commission of Assembly that its representatives who had been sent to Raasay had been kept waiting for between three and four hours because Mr. Macfarlane had refused to give up the keys of the church (*The Scotsman*, 10 August 1893). The Presbytery of Lochcarron fared no better when it sent a deputation to Mr. Macdonald's congregation at Shieldaig; nor did the Presbytery of Dunoon when it sent a similar mission to the congregation of Kilfinan, which, though without a minister, had also decided to separate.

When these proceedings were reported, a majority of the Commission of Assembly felt sufficiently aggrieved to enforce the provisions of the Model Trust Deed against the dissenting congregations, and both Mr. Macfarlane and Mr. Macdonald were deprived of their churches and manses. This action was of course within the strict letter of the law, but it was carried out with a degree of insensitivity which brought the Church little credit and left a legacy of ill feeling which was to linger long after the immediate cause of the separation had been removed. A particularly unfortunate circumstance was that, since the proceedings had to be brought through Presbyteries, the names of some constitutionalist ministers – themselves firmly opposed to the Declaratory Act – appeared as prosecuting parties. Inevitably, this helped to drive a further wedge between the separating party and the remaining constitutionalists, and to aggravate a situation which was already fraught with difficulty. The division thus caused among those who had formerly been brethren was one of the saddest consequences of the Declaratory Act, and one for which the majority in the Church bore the prime responsibility.

Essentially, the viewpoints of both parties towards the Declaratory Act were at one. Both regarded it as an unjustifiable attempt by the majority to loosen the terms of subscription to the confessional standards of the Church. The difference between them lay in their view of the response called for. The Free Presbyterians took the view that the constitution of the Church had been fundamentally vitiated by the Act. They believed that the Act had effectively subverted the status of the Confession of Faith as the Church's chief subordinate standard, and that, to avoid association with the evils that would follow, the only recourse was to separate from the Church. The remaining constitutionalists, many of whom were to form the Free Church of 1900, took an essentially similar view of the Act. It has been argued on their behalf that, since the Questions and Formula put to ministers at their ordinations and inductions remained unaltered, the Act was in effect a dead letter. It was certainly the case that the Declaratory Act in the Free Church had not been followed through in the same way as its counterpart in the United Presbyterian Church, where ordinands were required to answer the Questions and subscribe the Formula 'in view of the explanations contained in the Declaratory Act' (*Rules and Forms of Procedure of the United Presbyterian Church*, 1895, p. 144). However, it would be unwise to press this argument too far. In their Reasons for Dissent at the passing of the Declaratory Act in 1892 the Free Church constitutionalists specifically stated that the Act 'must be regarded as a new law of this Church, which alters the relations of the Church to the Confession of Faith, by substituting for the doctrines therein embodied the statements made in the Act, as the future standard of orthodoxy in this Church' (Minutes of Free Church General Assembly, 1892). The argument that no change had been made in the Questions and Formula is in any event something of an academic one, since the Assembly of 1894, in what was presented as a relieving Act, stated that 'those who are licensed or ordained to office in this Church, in answering the Questions and subscribing the Formula, are entitled to do so in view of the said Declaratory Act'. Thus, though the Questions and Formula themselves were unchanged, the facility for an ordinand to take advantage of the Declaratory Act when answering and subscribing them was specifically written into the law of the Church.

It is best therefore to look elsewhere for a satisfactory vindication of the constitutionalists' position. They were as opposed to the Declaratory Act as their brethren who had separated; and by petition, overture and dissent they had made abundantly plain their dislike of the Act. But they did not see it, of itself, as requiring or indeed justifying separation from the Church. Indeed, believing as they did that the action of the majority had been unconstitutional, they saw it as their duty to stand by the Church and her constitution. They saw no reason why they should be forced out of the Church by the illegal proceeding of the majority. They did not believe that the Supreme Court of the Church had the power to alter the constitution in the face of a dissenting minority who adhered to it. And, so long as the avenue of dissent remained open, they were able to conserve their consciences and to avoid the discord and divisiveness which separation would cause. Indeed, if there was to be a separation, they judged that it should be seen to be brought about by those who had abandoned the constitution – as the majority, in their view, had undoubtedly done. And in this they were to be amply vindicated by the House of Lords judgment of 1904.

The difference between the two sides' response to the crisis was thus essentially a matter of judgment. Each response served its purpose. By publicly separating from the Church, Mr. Macfarlane and his supporters brought into prominence, in a very emphatic way, the strength of popular feeling in the Church, and especially in the Highlands, against the Declaratory Act. By remaining in the Church under dissent, the bulk of the constitutionalists preserved the identity of the Disruption Church and secured its continued title to the estate which was its due. The situation was well summed up by the Rev. George Mackay on his reception into the Free Church in 1905. He did not regret, he said, that he separated from the Free Church in 1893; he could not do otherwise. According to his conviction he could not then be a consistent Free Churchman without becoming a Free Presbyterian. But he could see how, in the Providence of God, it had come about that if all had acted as he did, 'then the decision on the Statute Book would not have been found there' (*The Monthly Record of the Free Church of Scotland*, January 1906). And others were to see things from the same perspective.

THE STRUGGLE FOR SURVIVAL

That the Declaratory Act had been intended as a stepping-stone towards Union was soon made abundantly clear. The subject of Union was reintroduced to the Free Church Assembly in 1894, and enthusiastically received. Pro-Union resolutions were adopted by successive Assemblies, and in 1897 formal negotiations were entered into between Committees of the two Churches. The work proceeded smoothly; the United Presbyterians for their part had nothing to lose and so were solidly behind the Union proposals. In the Free Church Assembly the constitutionalists opposed the moves at every step, though their ranks were increasingly thinned by death and defection. The most noted of those in the latter category was the Rev. Murdo MacAskill of Dingwall, who in 1897 succumbed to the blandishments of Principal Rainy and thenceforward supported the movement he had so long opposed. But there was a resolute core of loyalists determined to carry on the fight to the end. By 1900, when the uniting Act finally came before the Assembly, they were able to muster only 27 votes against 643 for the passing of the Act. But they had abundant confidence in the rightness of their cause; and, when the majority withdrew to consummate the Union, they put in hand carefully-rehearsed plans to continue the testimony of the Free Church. It was from the start an uphill struggle. The fabric of a church organisation had largely disappeared; resources were few, and severely stretched; and public opinion was generally hostile. In addition, the attitude of the majority – now constituted as the United Free Church of Scotland – was utterly uncompromising. Not an inch of houseroom were they prepared to grant to those who had been their fellow-ministers and fellow-worshippers in the Free Church. In a number of cases where congregations and ministers had adhered to the Free Church the majority raised legal actions seeking to have them removed from the buildings. Strong feelings were aroused in several areas, and in some cases the threat of civil disorder was only narrowly averted. Such was the turbulent issue of the much-vaunted Union which had aimed to heal the divisions of non-established Presbyterianism in Scotland.

The Free Church minority had made it plain before 1900 that, if the Union went ahead, they would not hesitate to assert their rights to the property. They lost no time in making good their word. On 14 December 1900 – little more than six weeks after the Union – an action on behalf of the minority was raised in the Court of Session. The essential aim of the action was to have the minority identified as the rightful successors to the Free Church of 1843, and therefore entitled to the rights and properties of the pre-1900 Church. In support of their case, the minority asserted that the new post-Union Church had departed in essential points from the original principles of the Free Church. Foremost among these was the establishment principle. This of course had been seen at an earlier stage as a potential barrier to Union, but the Uniting Act had merely left it an open question. Again, the minority claimed that, in adopting the Declaratory Acts of the Free and United Presbyterian Churches, and altering the Questions and Formula, the new Church did not embody the Confession of Faith as part of its constitution and so had abandoned a fundamental principle of the Disruption Church. On these two points – elaborated by written and oral evidence of painstaking length and complexity – the case for the future of the Free Church was to revolve.

The first judgment in the case was given by Lord Low, the Lord Ordinary in the Court of Session, on 9 August 1901. It was distinctly unfavourable to the Free Church. Lord Low argued in effect that the establishment principle had not been a fundamental part of the constitution of the Church and that the Declaratory Act had been a proper exercise of the Church's powers under the Barrier Act. On these grounds, he awarded judgment to the United Free Church.

Undaunted by this reverse, the Free Church minority appealed to the Second Division of the Court of Session, where the case was heard by three appeal judges, Lord Kingsburgh, Lord Trayner and Lord Young. Their judgment, delivered on 4 July 1902, was even more unfavourable to the Free Church. They upheld Lord Low's view that the establishment principle had not been a fundamental part of the Church's constitution and that the Church had had power to alter its relation to the Confession under the Declaratory Act. Again, judgment was awarded to the United Free Church.

It was generally thought that, in the face of judgments so uniformly adverse, the minority would now give up the struggle. But having come thus far, and remaining convinced of the justice of their cause, they resolved on the ultimate course of appeal to the House of Lords. The legal proceedings had already been expensive, since the costs of the earlier hearing had been awarded against the Free Church, but funds for the appeal to the Lords were willingly subscribed and the case proceeded to its final resolution.

The hearing before the House of Lords started on 24 November 1903, and was heard over two weeks. However, before judgment could be given, one of the judges died, and the case was ordered to be reheard. The second hearing took place between 9 and 23 June 1904, and judgment was finally given on 1 August. The result was a memorable triumph for the Free Church. The minority's case was upheld by five of the seven judges, and the two earlier judgments were reversed with costs. Of particular note was the finding – on which the judgment mainly rested – that the establishment principle had indeed been a fundamental part of the Free Church's constitution, and the view of at least three of the judges that the Confession of Faith, an essential element of the Church of 1843, had effectively been abandoned by the United Free Church. The judges were also united in the view that the Barrier Act – under which the Declaratory Act of 1892 had been passed – could not be used to effect changes in the Church's constitution but was merely a procedural measure aimed at certain strictly limited purposes.

The most devastating indictment of the majority's case was delivered by the Lord Chancellor himself: 'The so-called union is not really a union of religious belief at all . . . It is not the case of two associated bodies of Christians in complete harmony as to their doctrine agreeing to share their funds, but two bodies, each agreeing to keep their separate religious views where they differ, agreeing to make their formularies so elastic as to permit persons to accept them according as their respective consciences will permit ... It becomes but a colourable union, and no trust fund devoted to one form of faith can be shared by another communion simply because they say in effect there are some parts of this or that confession which we will agree not to discuss, and we will make our formularies such that either of us can accept it. Such an agreement would not, in my view, constitute a Church at all, or, to use Sir William Smith's phrase, it would be a Church without a religion. Its formularies would be designed not to be a Confession of Faith, but a concealment of such part of the Faith as constituted an impediment to the Union' (R.L. Orr, *Free Church of Scotland Appeals*, 1904, p.571). In these eloquent words the spurious basis of the 1900 Union was ruthlessly exposed; and the minority's claim to be the true successors of the Free Church – in face of all the opprobrium they had had to suffer – was in the end fully vindicated.

The decision of the Lords was greeted with a predictable cry of outrage from the United Free Church. To none was the reverse so shattering as to Principal Rainy, who saw his long-cherished schemes for union threatened with disaster. With remarkable resilience, however, he was soon back in the fray. A Free Church writer – and no sympathiser with his position – was later to remark: 'The sight of the old man of well-nigh fourscore winters staggering to his feet after the tremendous blow of 1 August 1904, and addressing himself with unconquerable fortitude to the task of restoring the shattered energies of his Church, is one that compels admiration' (A. Stewart (with J.K. Cameron), *The Free Church of Scotland 1843–1910*, pp.54–5). And, as Principal Rainy had been the main architect of the Union, so he was to be the moving spirit in the clamour for redress which now echoed around the country. A great cry of protest was set up, and the United Free Church used every means it could to draw attention to its plight. Public opinion was mobilised, and influential voices petitioned the Government. At the same time, the Church mounted what was in effect a campaign of passive resistance against the House of Lords decision. Despite the judgment in favour of the Free Church, the United Free Church refused to give up any of the property without specific legal proceedings in each case, and the Free Church was thus obliged to apply for interdicts for every building it wished to possess. The United Free Church skilfully exploited this situation for its own ends. As each successive batch of interdicts was reported in the Press, there was conjured up the vision of a Church under persecution, its congregations turned out into the wilderness at the behest of a mere minority with the force of the secular law on their side. This was of course entirely spurious; the dispossessed United Free Church congregations had ample accommodation to resort to, in vacant churches or with neighbouring congregations, and in no cases did any hardship result. But the claims were good propaganda value nevertheless.

Eventually, the clamour of agitation had the desired result. In December 1904 the Government appointed a Royal Commission, with Lord Elgin as Chairman, to investigate all the circumstances and to report. At the same time it set up a Departmental Commission, under Sir John Cheyne, to agree joint occupancy arrangements between the Churches in advance of a permanent settlement. This latter arrangement was not a success; and in face of continued obstruction from the United Free Church side the Free Church withdrew from it after only a few weeks. The Royal Commission, meantime, proceeded speedily with its work and issued its findings on 19 April 1905. These were reasonably predictable; the Free Church did not have the resources to manage the vast amount of property to which it had fallen heir, and a distribution of the property should be regulated by Parliament. To that end the report recommended the creation of an Executive Commission, with powers to allocate the property as it saw fit.

The Royal Commission's report found general favour in Scotland, despite understandable misgivings on the Free Church side. In a sense, of course, it proceeded on an unsafe legal principle, since it involved in practical terms setting aside the judgment of the highest Court of the land. But there was a general recognition that, in the situation in which the two churches found themselves, it offered the most practical solution to an otherwise intractable problem. For the United Free Church, of course, it was a welcome lifeline, offering the prospect of a legal title to at least a share of the disputed property. And even for the Free Church, there was the likelihood of undisputed possession in those areas where the Church was strong, and of relief from the burden of maintaining properties it did not need.

The Royal Commission's scheme was speedily endorsed by the

Government, and legislation to give it effect passed swiftly through Parliament. By the autumn of 1905, the Executive Commission was in operation. Chaired by Lord Elgin – who had also chaired the Royal Commission – it went studiously and carefully about its task, assessing congregational strengths in the disputed areas, hearing evidence, and holding local inquiries as it saw need. Its results, inevitably, were to allocate a majority of the property to the United Free Church. However, the Free Church was able to secure a very fair share of the property in those areas where its strength was greatest, and this proved generally adequate for its needs. It was of course a disappointment to see property lost to the Church which had been declared to be hers by the supreme Court in the land; and in years to come the decisions of the Commission were to have an inhibiting effect on the Church's growth in certain parts of the country. Perhaps the greatest blow was the loss of the New College and the Free Assembly Hall, which of course had a significance even beyond their practical use to the Church. In other cases, church buildings which had been reoccupied as a result of interdicts had again to be vacated. But, in general, the Commission's judgment was seen as reasonable and fair. The organisational needs of the Free Church were recognised, and a new Assembly Hall – the former Free St. John's Church – and College – the former Free Church Offices – were placed at her disposal. Thus equipped, the Church was ready for the task ahead.

ATTEMPTS AT REUNION

It is unfortunate from a number of respects that the property issue, vital as it was to the Church's future, has been allowed to obscure the no less important developments which were taking place in the Church in the immediate post-Union period. These events had mainly to do with matters of worship, practice and government, and their outcome was largely determinative of the Church's future identity.

In the immediate aftermath of the Union, the Church was of course chiefly absorbed in the struggle for survival and in coming to terms with the drastically altered circumstances in which she was placed. Necessarily in that situation, questions of organisation and readjustment took first priority. But, amid the turmoil of these early years, the Church did not allow herself to forget the reasons for her distinctive existence. Put in their simplest terms, these reasons derived from a stand against an incorporating Union which compromised the Church's testimony and her adherence to her confessional standards. It was particularly appropriate that at this juncture the Church should recall its association with those who, several years earlier, had felt obliged to separate from the pre-Union Church for similar reasons of doctrinal principle. In the intervening period, the Free Presbyterian Church had maintained a steady growth. New churches had been built, ministers settled, and a full church organisation formed. But the circumstances of 1893 had now changed; and to many in the post-Union Free Church it seemed both logical and reasonable that the two churches should now pool their resources in the interest of the testimony they both shared. Accordingly, at the meeting of the Free Church Commission of Assembly on 6 March 1901, overtures were tabled from the Presbyteries of Edinburgh and Glasgow seeking that moves be put in hand towards union. The Commission's response was to appoint a Committee, composed of several leading members of the Church, to confer with any similar Committee the Free Presbyterians might appoint to the same end; and at the General Assembly of 1902, this Committee was strengthened with the addition of several further members. The Church's initiative was considered by the Free Presbyterian Synod in July of the same year, but attracted no support. 'The Synod', the response ran, 'respectfully acknowledge receipt of an extract minute of the General Assembly of the Free Church of Scotland anent union with the Free Presbyterian Church, but considers the matter of union premature; declares its firm adherence to the position taken up by this Church in 1893, and its sense of the necessity of maintaining unimpaired the doctrines and principles set forth in the Deed of Separation, and further declares its willingness to receive any who may be ready to homologate the same' (*History of the Free Presbyterian Church of Scotland*, pp.99–100). When this discouraging message was reported to the Free Church Assembly in May 1903, little option was seen but to express regret at the outcome and to discharge the Committee. At the same time however the Assembly went on to 'declare afresh their friendly feeling towards that Church, and their readiness to give effect to that feeling whenever that is practicable in view of the circumstances in which many of the congregations of the two Churches find themselves in close neighbourhood' (Minutes of Free Church Assembly, 1903).

The failure of this initial approach was undoubtedly a disappointment for the Free Church. Viewed in retrospect, however, the outcome was scarcely surprising. Memories of the Declaratory Act controversy remained fresh, and in the eyes of the Free Presbyterians the post-Union Free Church still had to prove its credentials. In particular, the Church had to be seen to be taking action about the Declaratory Act. Claiming, as they did, to represent the Free Church of the Disruption, the Act undoubtedly formed part of their Statute Book; and, until it was removed out of the way, moves towards reunion on any meaningful basis were almost certainly doomed to failure.

Such moves, indeed, were already in hand, though they were proceeding slowly. At the General Assembly of 1901, in response to overtures from several Presbyteries, a Committee had been formed to consider the repeal of the Act and to report to the next Assembly. A draft Act for this purpose was approved by the Assembly of 1902, and sent down to Presbyteries for their consideration. But the Act had been defectively drafted, and when the returns from Presbyteries were considered it was found that it had failed to receive the necessary support. The Assembly of 1903 renewed the instructions to the Committee, and directed them to frame an acceptable Act in conjunction with the Church's legal advisers. The Assembly also however enlarged the Committee's remit to include matters concerning purity of worship and the ordination of deacons, and with this additional workload the Committee were not in a position to report their diligence until the Assembly of 1905. It had in any event been the advice of the law agents that, with the Church's law case now proceeding in the House of Lords, nothing should be done to rewrite the Church's statute book until the case had been determined. By the time of the 1905 Assembly that inhibition had been removed; and the repealing measure in its revised form was immediately enacted as an Interim Act. In the following year, after it had received the unanimous approval of Presbyteries, it was passed into the standing law of the Church.

The repeal of the Declaratory Act could reasonably be expected to have an impact on the Church's relations with the Free Presbyterian Church; and so, in a measure, it proved. At the Free Presbyterian Synod in July 1905, a motion was made to appoint a Committee to confer with representatives of the Free Church 'with a view to seriously considering the situation as between the two Churches in the best interests of the cause of Christ in Scotland' (*History of the Free Presbyterian Church of Scotland*, p.102). This did not however find favour with the majority in the Synod, who passed a counter motion pointing out continuing obstacles in the way of union. At the next Synod meeting in November, it was again proposed that discussions take place with the Free Church, to include the points on which the Synod had expressed concern at the earlier meeting. This was again rejected by the majority, and the objections to union reaffirmed. As a result, three ministers – Rev. John Macleod of Kames, Rev. Alexander Stewart of Edinburgh and Rev. George Mackay of Stornoway – abandoned their connection with the Free Presbyterian body and sought admission to the Free Church. This was gladly granted, and at a special meeting of the Commission of Assembly on 19 December 1905 the three ministers were formally received into the Church. All three were to attain distinction in their new sphere of service – Mr. Macleod, later Dr. Macleod, as a Professor in the Free Church College and a much-loved Principal of the College; Mr. Stewart, later Dr. Stewart, as minister of Free St. Columba's Church, Edinburgh; and Mr. Mackay, who later moved to Fearn, in Ross-shire, as one of the Free Church's most noted preachers.

In admitting these brethren, the Free Church gave particular attention to the alleged obstacles to union which had been stated by the Free Presbyterian Synod, and which had also troubled the minds of those who eventually joined the Church. The first of these concerned a statement in the preamble to the Act passed by the 1905 Assembly repealing the Declaratory Act of 1892. The offending section reads: 'Whereas this Church adheres, as she has always adhered, to her subordinate standards in terms of the Act of 1846 anent Questions and Formula'. It was alleged by the Synod that the words 'as she has always adhered' contained an implicit censure on the Free Presbyterian separation of 1893, since, if true, they rendered that separation unnecessary. Indeed, the Synod argued, they tended to fix the Churches in their present positions (*ibid*, p.103). The Free Church's response to this charge was unequivocal. When receiving the three Free Presbyterian ministers, the Commission gave them 'the definite assurance that by the use of the words 'as she has always adhered' in the preamble to the Act repealing the Declaratory Act of 1892, and relative legislation, this Church meant no more than to evince that while the Declaratory Act had been passed against the will and in face of the repeated dissents and protests of those who now form the Free Church, the Act of 1846 which regulated the Questions and Formula remained intact, and that she had no intention whatever of reflecting upon the action of the Free Presbyterian Church, but that on the contrary she regards the testimony raised by the Free Presbyterian Church in 1893 on behalf of Disruption principles as identical with her own' (Minutes of Free Church Commission of Assembly, December 1905). This was calculated of course not only to satisfy the three brethren who were being admitted, but also to justify the Free Church's position in the eyes of the Synod. The assurance was generous, and as ample as could have been given; and there can be no doubt that no slight to the Free Presbyterians was intended by the framers of the Act. At the same time, it must be admitted that the words do admit of a degree of ambiguity; and it is unfortunate that what appears to have been intended as no more than a gloss should have proved over the years to be one of the major impediments to closer relations between the churches.

The second difficulty advanced by the Free Presbyterian Synod was the uncertainty of the Free Church's position as regards the infallibility of Scripture. Here, the Synod made it plain that they were referring to a case which had agitated the Free Church itself over the previous months, and caused it no little embarrassment. The case concerned Dr. W. Menzies Alexander, who had been admitted from the United Free Church in 1903 and been appointed to the Chair of Divinity in the Free Church College by the Assembly of 1904. In 1902, before his admission to the Church, Dr. Alexander had published a book under the title *Demonic Possession* which to some readers appeared to incline towards a rationalistic view of certain of the miracles recorded in the New Testament. The views in the book were not widely known at the time of Dr. Alexander's admission to the Chair, and they were only brought to light when the United Free Church, in its official magazine, sought to exploit them for its own ends. A considerable agitation followed, and pressure grew for the Church to take action. To many, it seemed that the spectre of the Higher Criticism had returned to haunt the Church. Concern in the Highlands – the Free Church heartland – was particularly strong. At their meetings in the Spring of 1905, the Synods of Ross and of Sutherland and Caithness – representing a major area of the Church's strength – sent up overtures to the General Assembly asking that suitable action be taken. When the Assembly met, it was discovered that the agitation had had the desired effect, and that Professor Alexander had agreed to withdraw the book from circulation. However, the form in which the announcement was made left much to be desired; for it was merely stated that the book had been withdrawn 'in deference to the requirements made in various parts of the Highlands' (*Monthly Record of the Free Church of Scotland*, June 1905). This was, not without some demur, accepted by the Assembly; and there the matter was allowed to rest. No attempt, apparently, was made to persuade Professor Alexander to withdraw his opinions, as opposed to merely withdrawing the book from circulation; nor indeed did he volunteer to do so. The impression was therefore left that the Free Church was prepared to tolerate an interpretation of Scripture which rested on something less than complete infallibility, and it was to this that the Free Presbyterian Synod had particularly adverted.

On this point, too, the Free Church Commission of Assembly thought it necessary to affirm the Church's position very distinctly when admitting the three Free Presbyterian ministers in December 1905. 'The Commission', they stated, 'hereby give the brethren of the Free Presbyterian Church the definite assurance that this Church holds by and adheres to the infallibility, inerrancy and entire perfection of the Scriptures of the Old and New Testaments as of Divine authority, and that in accepting the Confession of Faith, her office-bearers are individually taken bound to assert, maintain and defend these truths, and that no known departure from their obligation to do so, in profession or in practice, is or will be tolerated' (Minutes of Free Church Commission of Assembly, December 1905). And, as if to redeem his indiscretion over his book, Professor Alexander himself addressed the Commission in terms calculated to remove any vestige of doubt. 'Take away from me the utter infallibility of Scripture', he declared, 'and you take my all . . . I cherish as more precious than life itself, the absolute infallibility of the Word of God' (*Monthly Record of the Free Church of Scotland*, January 1906). Dr. Alexander was to go on to render signal service to the Free Church, retaining his Chair in the College until his death in 1929. A man of great humility despite his massive learning, he amply repaid the trust which the Church had placed in him in the difficult period following the Union. That he should have been associated with the failure of attempts to re-unify like-minded brethren was indeed unfortunate, but the responsibility for that failure was by no means wholly his.

The Commission of December 1905 had one more piece of work to do before it finished its labours. Eleven years earlier, the two founding ministers of the Free Presbyterian Church had been evicted from their churches and manses, and the memory of those proceedings still rankled with many. Now that closer union was being sought, the time was judged right to make restitution. This the Commission did by stating, on behalf of the Church as a whole, 'the sympathy prevalent throughout her borders with the Rev. Donald Macfarlane, formerly of Raasay, now of Dingwall, who, with the late Rev. Donald Macdonald, Shieldaig, was excluded from his Church buildings in the year 1894, and her regret on account of the harsh judicial proceedings whereby the evictions of these two brethren and their congregations were effected' (Minutes of Free Church Commission of Assembly, December 1905). This statement, unsolicited as it was, was particularly welcomed by the three ministers who were joining the Church. One of them, Rev. Alexander Stewart, was later to write: 'It may seem a small matter from certain points of view, but the Free Church has seldom risen to a higher plane of Christian dignity' (A. Stewart (with J.K. Cameron), *The Free Church of Scotland 1843–1910*, p.85). It was another decade before the question of relations with the Free Presbyterian Church was to be revived, but the Commission's declaration was to remain on permanent record as a statement of the view of the Free Church on a particularly unfortunate episode in her history.

TURMOIL AND RECOVERY

The standard of the Free Church was carried through the crisis of 1900 by a small band of 26 ministers, almost all of them in Highland charges. In the years immediately following the Union, the ministerial strength of the Church was augmented by admissions from other churches, some of them Highland expatriates, and others young licentiates who, on completion of their college courses, decided to throw in their lot with the Free Church. But this process was very gradual; and by the end of 1904 the ministerial complement of the Church still numbered no more than 40. However, with the decision of the House of Lords in favour of the Free Church, the relative trickle of admissions to the Church became a flood. Decisions on admissions were, as a general rule, delegated to the Commission of Assembly, which had power to dispose of applications as it saw fit. Between November 1904 and March 1906 the Commission admitted some 20 applicants, either as ordained ministers or probationers. The denominational backgrounds of these men varied widely – some were ministers of the pre-1900 Free Church seeking readmission; others were members of Presbyterian

Churches overseas; still others were Congregationalists or Independents.

But the most significant inflow to the Free Church during this period was from a source which could not be regulated by the General Assembly or its Commission. Under a Mutual Eligibility Act of 1873 – the principles of which went back to pre-Disruption days – ministers of the English and Irish Presbyterian Churches were eligible for call to Free Church charges on the same basis as ministers of the Free Church itself. This arrangement had been drawn up at a time when the doctrinal testimony and standards of the two churches had been in close sympathy with that of the Free Church; but in the intervening period both the English and Irish Churches had undergone a process of change similar to that in the pre-1900 Free Church. As a result, those joining the Free Church from the English or Irish Presbyterian Churches had been exposed to influences which were not in every way compatible with the doctrine and practice of the Free Church. Accessions from the Irish Presbyterian Church were particularly numerous, both of ordained ministers and students. That these men, and their counterparts from other churches, were prepared to accept Free Church charges was certainly a mark of their general sympathy with the Church; but experience was to show that the accretion of such a significant body of outside support, grafted on to a relatively small denomination, was not in the long-term interest of the Church as a whole.

By the end of 1906 the ministerial strength of the Church, augmented by the new arrivals, had grown to over 70. At the same time, the number of students for the ministry had grown to 26 from only 2 in 1904. Not all the congregations could call ministers, and some of those admitted from elsewhere were never settled in charges. But their presence in such numbers had a fundamental effect on the character of the Church. The relatively close-knit, homogeneous Church of 1900 had given way to a more broadly-based body, united certainly on the fundamentals, but open to diversity of opinion on distinctive points of Free Church testimony on which, but a few years earlier, unanimity of view had prevailed.

The new developments were viewed with apprehension by not a few in the Church. Professor Colin Bannatyne, one of the leaders of 1900, gave expression to the growing concern when in his Report to the Assembly of 1907 he stated: 'Our Church pre-eminently requires peace within her own borders, and it would obviously be a grave menace to this being realised if men admitted from other churches to ministerial charges were not in hearty agreement with her determination to recede in no particular from Disruption ground'. Later in the same year Professor Bannatyne expressed himself even more strongly: 'Our people are entitled to demand, after the waves of trial which in quick and bitter and cruel succession have swept over their heads, that they should be freed from anxiety and agitation in regard to the permanence in their midst of the Disruption heritage for which they have sacrificed so much . . . and therefore we ought to show that it is our earnest desire to maintain in this Church the idea of the Disruption, that it should be a garden enclosed, and that it should not be a field open for importation from the four quarters of the globe of roots of bitterness which, springing up and bearing fruit after their kind, will inevitably produce grief and sorrow, tumult and trouble' (*Monthly Record of the Free Church of Scotland*, December 1907).

It was not only within the Free Church that the trend of affairs aroused comment. As early as April 1906 a United Free Church writer noted scornfully: 'There are found within her Baptists and Wesleyans who have a warm place in their hearts for hymns and organs, ministers English and Irish; preachers and teachers who failed to pass through the course of instruction that must be gone through ere men are ordained to the solemn office of the ministry according to the law and order of the Presbyterian Church of Scotland; office-bearers out of work, and Plymouth Brethren . . . Is this a body to be called the Free Church of 1843? Neither Dr. Chalmers nor Dr. Macdonald, Ferintosh, would confess that this is the Free Church of Scotland for which they suffered contempt, worldly loss and persecution' (*Highland Witness of the United Free Church of Scotland*, April 1906). In July of the same year *The Free Presbyterian Magazine* observed: 'It is perfectly plain there are men in the present Free Church who ought never to have been in it, and if the leaders had been faithful at the first, they would have been refused admission'.

That these views struck a chord with many in the Free Church was evident at the General Assembly of 1906 when several overtures were submitted from Presbyteries craving the repeal of the Mutual Eligibility Act. The Assembly of 1907 duly passed an interim Act, confirmed by the Assembly of 1908, stipulating that 'no minister or probationer of another denomination or church shall be received to the standing of a minister or probationer of this Church without the authority of the General Assembly or their Commission'. But while the mutual eligibility arrangement was thus brought to an end, its effects of course remained; and the Church was destined to pass through a period of turmoil before it could finally rid itself of what was later seen to have been a sadly misguided policy.

The crisis, when it came, centred around the question of purity of worship. It was scarcely surprising that men who had been nurtured, as many of them had, in an environment of hymns and instrumental music should find the Free Church form of worship austere and unattractive. Both hymns and instrumental music had been sanctioned in the pre-1900 Free Church; but the post-1900 Church, in an Act passed in 1905, had repealed the earlier legislation and restored the Church's worship to that practised at the time of the Disruption. For the majority of the Church, the Act merely reinforced existing practice; but in a small minority of congregations, accustomed to the laxer forms of pre-Union days, the Act proved decidedly difficult to enforce. Matters were not helped by the fact that these congregations were led by ministers imported from other Churches who were basically out of sympathy with the Free Church's stance on purity of worship. The results were not slow to show themselves. At Kinglassie, in Fife, the minister and his Kirk Session plainly demurred to defer to the requirements of the Act and were only brought into line after the intervention of the Commission of Assembly (Minutes of the Free Church Commission of Assembly, March 1906). In the case of the Free Elder Memorial Church, Leith, a much more serious situation arose. The minister, the Rev. James Watson, was a former Irish Presbyterian who had made clear his view that the 1905 Act was an unwarrantable constraint on the liberty of congregational praise and who was plainly prepared to carry his convictions into action. In this he was supported by the majority of his congregation.

In November 1907 the Commission of Assembly had drawn to their attention that instrumental music had been used in the Leith congregation, contrary to the clear instruction of the 1905 Act. A Committee of the Commission was appointed to investigate the situation, and to report to a later meeting of the Commission. The appointment of the Committee aroused strong feelings in the congregation, and when the members visited the Leith church, on 4 March 1908, they were physically obstructed by Mr. Watson's supporters and subjected to various forms of petty harassment (Free Church Assembly Reports, 1908). The Commission took so grave a view of these proceedings that they reported them in full to the General Assembly. The issue had meantime reached the pages of the secular Press, and was being hailed by the enemies of the Free Church as an evidence of the internal tensions in the Church and even as a sign of its impending disintegration.

The Leith case, as it came to be known, was rendered even more intractable by the fact that one of the senior elders in the congregation was Mr. John Hay Thorburn, General Secretary of the Free Church and Depute Clerk of the General Assembly. A son of a former Free Church minister, Mr. Thorburn had played a leading part in the events leading up to the Union and since 1900 had occupied a highly influential position in the Church. No one had been more active than he in the events surrounding the House of Lords case and in the subsequent negotiations with the Elgin Commission. In a very particular way, he acted as the spokesman for the Free Church. With his acute legal mind, he was often more than a match for the spokesmen of the opposing side; and there can be no doubt that in the testing circumstances of the immediate post-Union years he rendered the Church signal service.

But while his administrative talents were beyond dispute, Mr. Thorburn's perception of the ethos and identity of the Church was seriously open to question. This did not emerge as a difficulty in the years immediately following 1900 when the Church was preoccupied with pursuing her legal rights; but when matters of doctrine and practice came under closer review, from around 1905 onwards, his divergence from the mainstream opinion in the Church became increasingly apparent. Despite all his contendings for the Free Church Mr. Thorburn appeared to set relatively little store by the great doctrinal issues which were at the forefront of the testimony of 1900. For him the Free Church was to be considered in terms of the Disruption ideal of a national Church, with its doors open to all, carrying its testimony into all quarters of the land. This was of course a noble ideal, and one for which Chalmers and others had contended; but to place it as a priority in 1900, as Mr. Thorburn wished to do, was to take no account of the changed spiritual climate in Scotland since 1843. It was that changed climate which had given rise to the defection inherent in the Declaratory Act, and which had drawn forth the testimonies of 1893 and 1900. The measures taken to conserve the Church's purity of worship and the standards of its ministry were of course designed to safeguard the testimony, and to prevent a relapse into the ways of the pre-1900

Church. But Mr. Thorburn did not see them in that light; to him they were man-made restrictions on the Church's original mission. He particularly deplored what he saw as the Highland or 'Celtic' domination of the post-1900 Free Church and the consequences of this for the Church's witness in the contemporary world. Issues such as materials of praise, and postures in public worship, were, he believed, being determined by Highland cultural tradition rather than by Scriptural standards. And in restricting entry to its ministry – and particularly debarring entrants from the Irish Presbyterian Church, unless formally admitted – the Church was deliberately isolating itself from the mainstream of the Christian community.

There can be no doubt that Mr. Thorburn's view of the Church, in the era immediately following 1900, was untypical of the Church as a whole. But in his influential position as General Secretary he was able to direct the affairs of the Church in such a way as to conform to the vision he had in mind, and to divert the course of the Church into channels increasingly opposed to the will of the majority. There is evidence that he encouraged the inflow of ministers and students from the Irish Presbyterian Church, whom he saw as sympathetic to his views, and who were settled in increasing numbers before the loophole of the Mutual Eligibility Act was finally closed. It was one of those ministers who was settled in Mr. Thorburn's own congregation in 1905, and who, as has been seen, was to prove particularly troublesome over the principle of purity of worship.

By 1907, these issues were causing such concern that several overtures were presented to the General Assembly asking that the whole question of the status of officials in the Church be enquired into, and the structures of the Church brought more into line with Presbyterian principles. Though presented in this way, the overtures were clearly directed to minimising Mr. Thorburn's role in the Church, and to repairing the damage his policies had caused. The Assembly thought sufficiently seriously of the matter to refer it specifically to its Commission, with instructions to report. By this time, the presence of younger ministers unfamiliar with the Church's testimony was causing increasing tension. The Presbytery of Edinburgh, where several of these ministers had settled, was the scene of continuing friction and in March 1908 had to be admonished by the Commission to conduct its business in a manner more befitting a Christian assembly (Minutes of Free Church

Commission of Assembly, March 1908). There was evidence that other parts of the Church might be affected in the same way.

Against this background, the General Assembly of 1908 was a critical event in the post-1900 Free Church. Apart from the 'Leith case', which had already gained some notoriety, the Assembly was to consider the recommendations of its Commission on the status of officials and their future impact on the life of the Church. Not surprisingly, the Assembly was awaited with anticipation. Its outcome was seen in many quarters as determinative of the future course and identity of the Church.

To its credit, the Assembly faced the challenge with resolution. In face of a recommendation that Mr. Thorburn continue in office, a majority in the Assembly carried a motion terminating the post of General Secretary and awarding Mr. Thorburn a severance payment of £1,000. When the report on the Leith case came to be heard, a similar majority passed a motion of censure on Mr. Watson and his Session – Mr. Thorburn included – and ordered immediate action to enforce compliance with the laws of the Church. At the same time, the Assembly approved the terms of a draft Act strongly reinforcing the Church's commitment to purity of worship, and ordered that it be sent down to Presbyteries for their consideration.

The outcome of the Assembly was decisive. It showed clearly that the Church was determined to brook no interference, even from the most influential sources, in its standards of worship and government. For Mr. Thorburn, it marked the end of his association with the Church. His parting shot was to publish a vitriolic pamphlet, which he assiduously circulated, and which gained a wide publicity. In it, he talked of the 'tradition and prejudice of a narrow and inconsequent party overpowering the experience and comprehensiveness of the Lowlands'; of a 'new Celtic sect with a man-made ritual of its own shrinking gradually in its isolation'; of a Church characterised more and more by 'self-righteousness and the exaltation of uniformity and authority of mere human majorities and traditions' (J. Hay Thorburn, *The Church of 1843 versus a new Celtic Free Church*, 1908).

That such views should have been held by one who held high office in the Church was disturbing enough; still more so was its potential for damage to the Church's witness and to its relations with those in other communions who shared its basic testimony. There can be little doubt, for example, that the outworking of these views seriously compromised the Church's credibility in the eyes of the Free Presbyterian Church, and consequently the prospects for reunion. They also, of course, seriously misinterpreted the Church's contendings at the time of the Union and earlier. It had not been the Church's intention, as Mr. Thorburn appeared to believe, to set herself up as a focal point for the revival of the Presbyterian cause in Scotland. Rather was she concerned to preserve undiluted the testimony and standards of the Free Church of 1843 – an aim which was amply vindicated by the House of Lords judgment of 1904. That testimony consisted in large part of an unqualified adherence to the Westminster standards, which of course had been at the centre of the Declaratory Act controversy a decade earlier.

In denigrating the Highland influence in the Church, Mr. Thorburn appears to have forgotten that it was Highland opinion which led the opposition to the Act – against which he himself had dissented at the 1893 Assembly. It was a facile conclusion that because the Highland element was dominant in the Church, the decisions reached by the Assembly on matters of worship and government had no higher authority than that of a mere cultural tradition. What such a view failed to recognise, or was unwilling to accept, was that over the previous half-century the focus of spiritual life in Scotland had moved indisputably from the south to the north; and it was in the Highlands, rather than the Lowlands, that the best elements of the Scottish Reformation heritage continued to survive. The notable revivals of the previous century, and the labours of a succession of worthy ministers, had produced a generation of solid and well-instructed Christians with a keen appreciation of spiritual truth. The Highland Christian was very conscious of his Reformed heritage. In particular, he shared the Reformers' high regard for the authority of Scripture and their view of the spirituality, and hence the simplicity, of New Testament worship. It was these principles which had determined the particular strength of Highland opposition to the dilution of the Church's confessional standards in 1892, and to the innovations introduced in the worship of the Church.

This then was the heritage into which the post-Union Free Church had entered. It was a heritage, certainly, geographically more circumscribed than in 1843, but grounded no less firmly in the Reformed tradition. The fact that in 1893 and 1900 the Church's testimony had been supported mainly in the Highlands, whereas in 1843 it had enjoyed broad support throughout Scotland, did not make it any less a testimony to Reformed truth. That was the basic fact which appeared to elude Mr. Thorburn and his supporters, or which they showed an unwillingness to grasp.

Against that background, it is not surprising that the Highland majority in the post-1900 Church showed a determination to conserve the principles of worship and practice which by then had become largely identified with the Highlands. They did not wish to turn the Free Church into the preserve of a particular culture. But they were conscious that, within that culture, there had been preserved something of inestimable value. And they were determined, for the sake of succeeding generations, that that testimony would not be lost.

It was that determination, reflected as it was in the outcome of the 1908 Assembly, that was largely decisive in moulding the future identity and character of the Church. Two years later, in 1910, the overture regarding public worship which had been agreed in principle in 1908 was passed formally into the law of the Church. Comprehensive in its scope, it reaffirmed in unequivocal terms the Church's commitment to purity of worship and its determination to resist all unscriptural innovations. To underline the importance of the subject, the Assembly ordered that the Act be read in public at all future ordinations and inductions of ministers. This requirement was to remain in force until 1932, by which time the Church's position on the subject was well understood. But to this day the substance of the purity of worship principle is required to be explained as part of the procedure at ordinations and inductions.

There was another Act of the 1910 Assembly which was significant for the Church's practice. This concerned the attitudes to be adopted in public worship. For centuries, worshippers in the Scottish Reformed Church had been accustomed to stand at prayer. However, in later Victorian times there had been an increasing prevalence to pray seated. The Free Church now restored the Reformation practice, which, the Act declared, was 'sanctioned by Scripture and authorised by this Church, and the reverence due to the professed worship of God'. It also stated that 'inasmuch as there is no such guidance in the matter of praise, it is expedient, having regard to the comfort of worshippers, that the posture in praise be that of reverent sitting in the pew'. There is not a little evidence to suggest that here, too, the Act faithfully reflected Reformation practice. Again, therefore, there is no ground to see in either of these practices any relic of a mere cultural tradition.

With the course of the Church now firmly settled, there was

diminishing room for those who had wanted to turn it into a different direction. The effects were not slow to appear. In November 1909 the Rev. James Watson and his Kirk Session formally resigned from the Church, and in 1910 Mr. Watson was received into the Church of Scotland. Others soon followed. Between 1910 and 1920 some 30 ministers resigned from the Church, of whom the greater part joined the Church of Scotland. The majority of these were younger men who clearly found themselves out of sympathy with the course on which the Church was now settled. Their departure weakened the ranks of the ministry, but not the Church's testimony. And, with increasing numbers of students coming forward from within the Church's own ranks, the gaps left were steadily filled.

With the Church restoring herself once again to the pattern of 1900, it was natural that thoughts should return to cultivating close relations with the Free Presbyterian Church, which had continued to pursue its separate way. In August 1916, apparently in response to encouragement received, the Free Church Commission of Assembly appointed a Committee to confer with any similar Committee appointed by the Free Presbyterian Church 'on all matters that may at present be regarded as obstacles to co-operation or union'. When the Free Presbyterian Synod considered this initiative at its meeting in 1917 it drew up a 'Statement of Differences' which it saw as impediments to union, and transmitted this to the Free Church (*History of the Free Presbyterian Church of Scotland*, pp.121–2). The fact that the Synod responded in this way was seen by the Free Church as a positive step, since it enabled the issues to be addressed and debated, though the statement itself was in uncompromising terms. Of the six 'Differences' the first two were well-trodden ground – the affair of Professor Alexander's book and the preamble to the 1905 measure repealing the Declaratory Act. The others were concerned respectively with the indiscriminate admission of ministers to the Free Church; the prevalence of 'church bazaars and sales of work, church soirees and social meetings' within the Church; the Church's practice of allowing prayers at the graveside; and its slowness in removing a 'Popish symbol' from one of its churches. (The reference here was to a memorial window in the Lochranza Free Church in Arran, which depicted a figure of Christ; the window had been installed by the widow of a Glasgow councillor who had close connections with Lochranza and the Free Church's efforts to remove it had received wide publicity in the Press). All these matters were reasonably predictable; they had already been the subject of critical comment in the official magazine of the Free Presbyterian Church and had also, in varying degrees, been the cause of anxiety within the Free Church itself.

The Synod's statement was rightly given due priority, and in November 1917 the Commission of Assembly approved a full and detailed reply. Framed in courteous and conciliatory terms, it expressed the Commission's joy that the Synod's statement 'discloses nothing in the professed creed of either Church that should warrant their continued separation'. The reply went on to deal with the Synod's statement point by point. On the question of Professor Alexander's book and the preamble to the Act it repeated the assurances given in 1905, in even stronger terms. Professor Alexander had, it claimed, 'frankly expressed his regret for any reflections which the book was fitted to cast on the infallibility of the Word of God'; and the Commission, the reply went on, 'regret whatever hurt was done to truth and the religious beliefs and feelings of God's people within and without the Church by certain views expressed in the book referred to'. On the preamble to the Act, the reply pointed out that while the Declaratory Act of 1892 had been '*de facto* and *de forma* an Act of this Church' it could not be considered an Act *de jure*; accordingly, the reply went on, 'the Church reaffirms solemnly that the phrase in the Rescinding Act – 'as she has always adhered' – does not, in the light of ascertainable data, imply, and was not intended to imply a censure on the Free Presbyterian Church, but was intended, and is hereby declared, to bear, only the construction of recording an historical fact that this Church did, under the above-named conditions, adhere, as she now does under freer circumstances adhere, to her subordinate standards in terms of the unchanged Questions and Formula of 1846; but, in the event of union between the two Churches being consummated on the basis of 1843, this statement would consequently disappear, and the United Church would not in any way be held responsible for it'.

On the admission of ministers, the Commission owned 'that it is admitted, and has to be regretted, that some ministers and students entered the Church through the previously-existing avenue of the Mutual Eligibility Act (now repealed) and otherwise, who found themselves out of full sympathy with her testimony and consequently left her communion'. The Commission however went on to affirm 'that of recent years such vigilance has been observed in the important matter of admission of ministers and students as can be claimed by any Evangelical church in the land, as is witnessed by the searching set of questions now put to all such aspirants'. On social functions and the like, the Commission saw the 'providing of amusements' as incompatible with 'the Scripturally-defined functions of the Christian Church' and maintained that the Free Church 'emphatically condemns these in so far as they are inconsistent with the solemnity and serious requirements of the Christian ministry and the Christian life and conduct'; however, 'to avoid excess or defect in all respects' the Commission proposed discussions with the Free Presbyterians 'on these and any other matter which, if left undetermined, might be a source of irritation in a united body'. The Commission finally turned to the questions of prayer at the graveside and the 'Popish symbol' in the Lochranza Church. On the former, it asserted 'that this Church in condemning everything and anything that savours of prayers for the dead, seeks to pay the same kind of respect to the Directory of Public Worship that was shown to it by our evangelical forefathers'; and on the latter, it maintained that 'the Church was for a time impeded in the exercise of her disciplinary power by legal questions affecting proprietary rights, but that particular difficulty now ceases to exist' (Minutes of Free Church Commission of Assembly, November 1917).

In the preamble to their reply, the Commission had expressed the view that the situation as regards union was 'now happily full of promise' and the reply to the Synod was despatched in that expectation. However, so far as any incorporating union was concerned, these hopes were doomed to disappointment. When the Synod met in July 1918 it passed a majority motion terminating the exchanges and dismissing the Free Church reply as 'largely made up of evasive statements and suggestions of compromise' (*History of the Free Presbyterian Church of Scotland*, pp.128–9). A minority however dissented from the Synod's finding, and at the Commission of Assembly in November 1918 three Free Presbyterian ministers – Rev. John R. Mackay of Inverness, Rev. Alexander Macrae of Portree and Rev. Andrew Sutherland of Lochbroom – were admitted to the Free Church. At the General Assembly of 1919, Mr. Mackay was appointed to the Chair of New Testament in the Free Church College, which he occupied until his retirement in 1935. Mr. Macrae became minister of Maryburgh Free Church, but sadly died within a year; while Mr. Sutherland exercised a long and useful ministry in a succession of charges until his retirement in 1951.

So ended the Free Church's attempt at dialogue between the two churches. From the human point of view, at least, it must remain matter for regret that closer contacts in the immediate post-Union days, which could have set the pattern for the future, were not found to be possible. From that point of view it is particularly unfortunate that there were found in the post-1900 Free Church practices to which discriminating Christians could legitimately take exception. This applies perhaps particularly to the question of 'social meetings'. The habits of pre-Union days sometimes proved hard to break, and accounts of congregational meetings in the early 1900s would surprise a modern Free Church reader. The indiscriminate admission of ministers from other churches, several of whom had no sympathy with Free Church principles, undoubtedly formed another stumbling-block to unity with those with whom the Free Church had a much greater affinity of outlook and interest. But by 1917 many of these difficulties were on the way to being resolved; and the Church's initiative at that time had been a sincerely-meant effort which had looked for a somewhat kindlier response. There were to be others later, with a similar result.

By the time the Church entered the 1920s, her course had been firmly charted for the future. She had passed through a particularly turbulent period in her history. She had endured external hardship and internal conflict. In the early years, she had had to fight for her very survival. Later, when the battle seemed won, she had had to resist a determined attempt to divert her on to a course of ecclesiastical syncretism which had proved the undoing of the post-Disruption Church. Now, two decades after the Union, her future course was clear. Certainly, she regretted the fragmentation of the Presbyterian witness in Scotland and would have rejoiced in a reunion which would have conserved the Reformation testimony. But she was not interested in union for its own sake, or as a mere external form. Nor was she prepared to trim her sails to the wind of ecclesiastical fashion, be it concerned with internal church order or wider denominational relations.

Rather was she concerned, as any true Church of Christ must be, in maintaining a testimony faithful to Scripture. Such a testimony had been raised in 1843, and again in 1893 and 1900. On each occasion, the Headship of Christ had been under threat. As heirs of the Disruption, the men of 1900 fully endorsed the testimony raised in 1843 for Christ's Headship over the Church. But to them had been committed, in a very particular way, a testimony inherent in that of 1843, to which they were now called upon to give distinctive expression. That testimony concerned the Headship of Christ over the doctrine and worship of the Church. In the Providence of God, the honour of conserving that testimony had fallen largely to a particular constituency of the Church; and that fact was faithfully reflected in the pattern of the Church of 1900. To be sure, the testimony was not the product of a particular culture. But events had shown that the cultural background was by no means irrelevant. Indeed, the Church had found by sad experience that the more she departed from the pattern of 1900, the less sure her grasp of her distinctive testimony became.

Twenty years after the Union, that pattern had been largely re-established. The composition of the Church's ministry once again resembled that of the immediate post-Union period. The commitment of her ministers to the testimony of the Church was unquestioned. Professor Bannatyne, who died in 1920, could claim to have lived to see the Church fulfilling the ideal of the 'garden enclosed' of which he had spoken in 1907. That was not to say, of course, that the Church had set herself up to be inward-looking or isolationist; indeed, she was fruitfully extending her witness both at home and overseas. But so far as her distinctive identity was concerned, the course of Providence had clearly taught her to see as normative the testimony she had been called upon to make in 1900, and the standards of worship and practice of which that testimony was the foundation. And it was on that ground that the heirs of the Disruption now took their stand as they looked to the future.

2

Church and State: Good Neighbours and Good Friends?

DAVID A. ROBERTSON

INTRODUCTION

'Thumbs Down for State Cash Offer' ran the headline in the *Christian Herald* newspaper on 31 March 1990. It was referring to the Federation of Evangelical religious bodies in Spain who had just rejected an offer of money raised from the Spanish system of charity taxes. Jose Cardona, a Baptist minister, stated: 'The State should not subsidise religion. Every Church which receives money from the state is compromised with the State'. A principled stand which many would agree with and admire – and yet a stand which the Free Church founders and the Protestant Reformers would undoubtedly call unbiblical and foolish. In this essay we shall see why. We shall look at the question of State–Church relations, attempt to see what the principles were that our forefathers saw as being so important, and examine the relevance of these principles for today.

If this essay had been entitled 'The relevance of the establishment principle for today' it would have been an accurate but off-putting title. It does not exactly promise riveting reading! But if we state that it is an essay about education, marriage, student grants, the monarchy, taxes, politics, deeds of covenant, evangelism and the poor – that also is accurate and gives a better idea of the scope and the importance of the subject in hand.

Many people do not realise that one of the fundamental beliefs of the Free Church of Scotland is the principle of the national establishment of religion. 'The Free Church of Scotland took its beginnings as such, over the Church–State issue – the spiritual independence of the Church and its claim to recognition and support by the State – and it regards that issue as being just as relevant and crucial now as it was then' (Neil Macleod, *Hold Fast Your Confession*, p.71). The House of Lords' judgment of 1904 found that the principle of the national establishment of religion is a fundamental tenet of the Free Church, based on chapter 23 of the Westminster Confession.

However in actual fact the Free Church, on the whole, does not see the relevance of the establishment principle today and despite the question put to ministers and elders before ordination about the Claim, Declaration and Protest of 1842, most of us have pushed it into the locker room of history. If that is the case in the Free Church it is also true in the wider Church and yet the principles which were fought over in 1843 are principles which can be of great assistance to the Christian Church today, as it seeks to work out its relationships to the various states that it finds itself in.

What do we mean?

For the purposes of clarity it is helpful to declare what we mean by the terms, Church and State. The Church is the visible organisation of the 'called out' people of God. It consists of all those who profess faith in the Lord Jesus Christ and their children and, in the Presbyterian set-up, is organised into local congregations governed by Kirk Sessions, presbyteries, synods and general assemblies. Its sole head is Jesus Christ.

The State is the government of human society, to enable that society to function. Its duty is to ensure that all its members are protected and provided for; to maintain order and peace and to do so by enforcing the rule of law. The establishment principle would teach that it is also the duty of the State to ensure that the Church has liberty to preach the Gospel and to encourage the Church in its task. In today's society the State often claims total order and sovereignty, the Church is often seen as a religious fringe group and the ideal relationship is seen by many as that of an all powerful secular state with the Church being a kind of private club within that State. This is the secular humanist approach rather than the Biblical one.

What does the Bible say?

The Bible has some very startling things to say to us about the Prime Minister, President, local MP or Councillor. It tells us that they have been established by God. 'The authorities are God's servants, who give their full time to governing' (Romans 13.6). This comes as something of a shock for those who have always assumed that the State is a 'bad thing' and that the true Church must always be aloof from, if not against the powers that be. Peter tells us that we are to submit ourselves 'for the Lord's sake to every authority instituted among men' (1 Peter 2.13). We are to give the authorities taxes, revenue, respect and honour. We are to give to Caesar what is Caesar's (Matthew 22.21). The State's authority then, like the Church's, is an authority given from God. The British Prime Minister, the American President, Saddam Hussein and your local Councillor are all responsible ultimately, not to the electorate, the military or themselves, but to God.

Furthermore we know that the message of the Bible is a message which has political effects. Jesus' message was political in that it affected the 'polis' the society in which he was living. He denounced corrupt rulers, preached good news for the poor, refused to be a military political leader and yet led a revolutionary movement. Therefore those Christians who regard the State as necessarily evil, and politics as nothing to do with the Christian, are being unfaithful to their Lord and ignoring His Word.

Most Christians recognise that the Bible does indeed speak of two powers – the power of the keys given to the Church and the power of the sword given to the magistrate. The difficulty is deciding how Church and State, Christianity and politics, relate to one another. As we look at this we would do well to bear in mind the words of Francis Schaeffer: 'The basic problem of the Christians in this country in the last eighty years or so, in regard to society, and in regard to government, is that they have seen things in bits and pieces instead of totals' (Francis Schaeffer, *A Christian Manifesto*, p.423).

HISTORICAL SURVEY

In the history of the Church of Jesus Christ there have been four different solutions offered to the problem of Church–State relations. The first, which is commonly known as Erastianism (after the 16th century Reformer, Erastus) teaches that the State is supreme and has control over the Church. This is the view that until the present century was held strongly by the British Monarchy and much of Parliament. When confronted with the claims of the Free Church regarding spiritual independence Queen Victoria replied 'most extraordinary and inadmissible' and her Prime Minister, Sir Robert Peel, argued that 'if patronage is abolished then nothing but evil will result'. The Moderates in the Church of Scotland before the Disruption were, in general, Erastian.

Peel and others were frightened of the second solution that has been offered – clericalism. That is where the Church dominates the State, as happened for example at the time of the Holy Roman Empire. Clericalism would desire the Church even to be supreme in civil matters. The third view of Church–State relations is the most popular view today, and that is strict separation. According to this view Church and State are entirely separate and must not interfere with one another. The final view, which we are seeking to defend, is the idea that Church and State each have their own area of competence and authority and that if circumstances are right there can be a great deal of cooperation between the two of them – without the one dominating the other.

To many people things were going along just nicely in the early Church until the Emperor Constantine professed faith in Christ. After his conversion, the theory goes, Christianity became the official religion of the Roman Empire and the Church became linked with the Roman State. The result was corruption coming into the once pure bride of Christ and the Church being saddled with the wrong understanding of Church–State relations until recently. This is the position taken, amongst others, by Dr Martyn Lloyd-Jones who argues that even Luther and Calvin did not go far enough in the Reformation. 'To me' he argues, 'one of the tragedies of the Reformation was the way in which Luther, Calvin and Zwingli tended to take over the notion of the State Church' (D.M. Lloyd-Jones, *Knowing the Times*, p.194). However such a view does not do justice to the historical facts, nor the fact that Luther, Calvin and others all thought that there could be a Biblical linkage between Church and State.

In AD 313 Constantine's edict of toleration did indeed make religion a matter of individual conscience, restored property to Christians and the Church and paid the clergy out of public funds. This in itself was not a bad thing – it did not usher in heresy (which had already reared its head in the Church from New Testament times). It did, however, have many dangers: dangers which are still with us whenever Christianity becomes popular. As the Emperor was a Christian there was a danger that others would profess faith in order to curry favour, and there was always the danger of clericalism (the Roman Church did eventually become a dominant political force) and of State control. The real disaster was not that the State supported the Church but rather that the Church began to take political power, which it had no right to. However, the fact that there were dangers does not mean that Constantine's edict of toleration was a bad thing. Some would argue that because the Church was small and persecuted there was better fellowship and so it should always stay that way. But what does happen when a ruler does 'kiss the Son' (Psalm 2) and when Christianity does become popular? Can a ruler govern in a Christian way? Can a state be so influenced by Christianity that it governs according to God's Word? Or do we believe that the Church will always be small and despised? There is danger in growth but does that mean the Church should not grow and have an impact upon the governments of the world?

At the time of the Reformation the Reformers did not divorce Church and State. They allowed the relationship to remain, removing not the machinery, but rather the people who were operating it. Calvin in particular expressed a Biblical doctrine of Church and State. The Calvinist states left religion generally with income and control over morals and doctrine, but not economic or political control. Calvin taught that the State must guarantee the Church freedom and her doctrine. He did not believe that it was the duty of either the State or the Church to enforce the civil Mosaic law of the Old Testament (ie stoning for adultery) but that it was the duty of the State to enforce the moral law and the precepts of love. The law, in Calvin's thought, was to be the same for all men everywhere – an important principle that we must never forget. Also in Calvin's teaching it was clear that Christians were to have a positive attitude towards politics and the State. 'For Calvin, the Scriptures teach that only the faith of Jesus Christ is to be accorded the positive support of the State. This is the essence of Christian civil government' (G. Keddie, 'Calvin on Civil Government', *SJET*, Spring 1985, p.33). 'We must always hold on to the principle that magistrates are appointed by God for the protection of religion and of the public peace and decency, just as the earth has been ordained to produce food' (Calvin, *Commentary on 1 Timothy*, p.204.)

Since the Reformation there have been different forms of Church–State relations in countries where the Christian faith has predominated. In England the partial reformation that occurred resulted in a Church which was tied too closely to the State – a Church in which the Monarch was both emperor and Pope. The exception to this was during the English Civil War and the resultant Commonwealth established by Oliver Cromwell and the Puritans in the 1650s. Parliament in 1648 set up a Presbyterian establishment with toleration for dissenting Protestant sects. It went beyond the bounds of its jurisdiction when it imposed the death penalty for disbelief in the physical resurrection and denial of the Bible as the Word of God. Belief cannot be imposed, nor dísbelief punished by any State. (Incidentally our Baptist brethren would not have been too pleased at Parliament's decision that the denial of infant baptism could also lead to imprisonment!) However, Cromwell, tired of the persecuting principles of some of the Parliament, sought to set up a truly national established tolerant Church. John Owen and a committee appointed by Cromwell envisaged a national established Church surrounded by self-supporting non-conformist churches, tolerated and recognised by the established Church. Owen and his committee laid down 15 fundamental doctrines that one had to believe in order to be a preacher in this national Church. This bold attempt was of course defeated with the restoration of the monarchy and the subsequent State domination of the Church.

At the other end of the scale, the Puritans and others, who left England for the New World in America, also set up a new pattern of Church–State relations. The American Constitution was the first to provide a wall of separation between Church and State. The First Amendment states that 'Congress shall make no law respecting an establishment of religion or prohibiting the free exercise thereof . . .' Despite the way that this is interpreted today it was not the case that there was no relationship between Church and State in the American colonies. Nine out of the thirteen States had laws conferring special benefits on the Church. Twelve of them taxed people to provide Gospel support and Churches. Nonetheless it is the case that in the American Constitution there is a fundamental separation of Church and State – which helps explain why, with the influence of American evangelicalism, this view of Church–State relations is so popular today.

In Scotland the situation has always been different – coming between the English and American models. From Knox, through Rutherford's *Lex Rex* to Thomas Chalmers, the Scottish Church has held to the model of the two powers, each supreme in its own sphere – each co-operating with one another. State and Church, both deriving their authority from God, are to be good neighbours and good friends. That is why, whenever the State encroached into matters which were the province of the Church, the Scottish Church opposed that and suffered for it. John Knox, Andrew Melville, the National Covenant of 1638, the Covenanters and the Disruption of 1843 all illustrate the fact that the Scottish Church, whilst being prepared to recognise the authority of the secular power, was also prepared to follow the higher authority when there was a conflict. King Jesus has priority over any secular power.

THE DISRUPTION

It is not the purpose of this essay to go into the history of the 1843 Disruption. However, if we are to apply the principle that was fought for then we must understand what it is. Some people have interpreted the momentous events of the Ten Years conflict as a political struggle – or as a time when the Church cast off the shackles of the Church–State doctrine and became free. In actual fact the Church of Scotland Free was formed holding firmly on to the principle of an established Church. It was prepared to leave the establishment because of the wrong attitude of the State, but it longed for a return to a pure establishment where the Church would be free and recognised and supported by the State. The most eloquent advocate of this was the most important leader of the Free Church of Scotland, Thomas Chalmers. In seeking to understand the relevance of the establishment principle for today it is necessary to return to the arguments presented by Chalmers over 150 years ago.

From April 25th to May 12th of 1838 Chalmers delivered a series of six lectures to an influential audience in London. These lectures had a great impact and were printed immediately, going through several editions. They remain a powerful argument for the establishment of national religion.

Chalmers' entire theory rested on a great compassion for the poor and a desire to see the Gospel spread. He argued that if there was only a voluntary system then the Church would basically become a middle-class institution. If Christianity was left to free-trade then there would only be religion where people would pay for it. He declared 'we do not sell the gospel – but offer it' (Chalmers, *Lectures on the National Establishment of Religion*, p.25). (It is undoubtedly a problem today in both Britain and America that the Church is very often seen as a middle-class institution.) Chalmers argued that if we wanted to see a Christian nation then the government should seek to provide support so that the Gospel could be taken to the poor. Chalmers, an arch Tory, insisted that contributions should be forced from the wealthy to help the poor. However, to Chalmers, the essence of establishment was not that the government provided financially for the Church, but rather that there should be a national recognition of true Christianity in law. The funding of the Church could still come privately.

To the government Chalmers pointed out the advantages of supporting the Church. If you have more Christianity you will have less money spent on soldiers, policemen and prisons. The advance of the Gospel will lead to better citizens. The State can only provide the machinery – the Church provides the Gospel. 'The Christian governor, after having laid down his parishes and planted his churches thereon, looketh for the descent of the blessing from above, without which the country will abide as hopeless a moral wilderness as before' (Chalmers, *ibid.*, p.5).

The advantages to the Church are also clear. The support of the government would enable a greater spread of the Gospel. To the riposte that this was using carnal weapons to fight spiritual battles Chalmers responded by pointing out that no matter whether the giving was voluntary or state, all it was providing was the machinery. We still needed the outpouring of God's Holy Spirit whatever our methods. To thrust home his point he used a series of powerful arguments.

If a Christian philanthropist gave money for Church, manse and salary – without conditions except that the minister be a Presbyterian – what would be the objection to accepting the money? And if the government were to do the same what would then be the objection? Why should not governments as well as individuals support the Gospel cause? If governments gave money for universities, schools, museums, then why not for Churches? There is no need for the Church to get its theology from the government – after all the State endows schools but does not tell them what to teach (a situation which has changed somewhat from Chalmers' day!). If the government did not spend now we would reap as a nation later.

To Chalmers the State supporting the Church would not involve compromise – because as soon as the State would seek to overstep its authority the Church would leave the establishment. 'There is not one thing which the State can do to our independent and indestructible Church but strip her of her temporalities' (Chalmers, *ibid.*, p.18). The relationship between Church and State is one of equality – 'We knock at the door of government, not in the crouching attitude of supplicants for ourselves, but in the firm and high attitude of donors ... and saying "this is our contribution; what is yours?"' (Chalmers, *ibid.*, p.43).

The actual application of the establishment principle at that time was seen by Chalmers to be relatively straightforward. The State was not to make the choice of which Church to support on a narrowly sectarian basis. He saw the decision as being one of supporting Roman Catholicism or Protestantism. There should be a national Protestant Church together with a toleration of Romanism (without actively supporting it). The voluntary churches were to supplement the establishment but they would not supersede it. The established Church would be responsible for a parish ministry, ensuring that every person had a right to be visited by a minister. The territorial–parish principle was fundamental to the working of Chalmers' plan.

Chalmers' theory was never put into practice because the State, with the collusion of the moderates in the Church, sought to reject the right of the Church to choose its own ministers and make its own ecclesiastical laws. The result was that, rather than give up the freedom of the Church of Christ, most of the evangelicals left the established Church of Scotland and formed the Church of Scotland, Free. Nonetheless they looked for better days when the prosperity of the Gospel would lead to a godlier nation. We should have the same vision.

The problem for us is not the arguments that Chalmers put forward (which are agreeable with Scripture and sanctified common sense) but rather the application. He applied the principle of 'good neighbours and good friends' – the principle of the government recognising and supporting true Christianity – in a different age from ours. If we are to resurrect the establishment principle from the graveyard of 19th century ecclesiastical history then we must seek practical ways to apply it in the modern world. It is the mutual co-operation model of Chalmers and the Westminster Confession which provides a radical and helpful basis for Church–State relations today – not only in our own country but also in countries where the Church is rapidly growing and where evangelicals are increasingly involved in government.

THE SITUATION TODAY

'The interaction between religion and politics and the necessity for a spiritual dimension in the life of any nation, make it essential to have a framework in which religious bodies relate to their State authorities' (Stewart Lamont, *Church and State – Uneasy Alliances*, p.5). Of that there can be no doubt. But what is the current situation as regards Church–State relations?

In America the Church–State separation has run into difficulties. The men who drew up the original constitution would be horrified at the way it is now being interpreted, particularly by the courts. This has now led to children not being allowed to pray in State schools, no nativity scenes, no copies of the ten commandments allowed in State schools, and the State has even attempted to enforce employment of homosexuals onto the Church. The State has gone so far as to make the theological moral pronouncement that a foetus does not become a human being on conception. In the infamous 1973 Roe v. Wade case the Supreme Court decided that it was illegal for individual states to outlaw abortion. The consensus that existed in previous centuries is now falling apart and a constitution which was designed to allow religious freedom and toleration may soon become an instrument of suppression for those who wish to practise their faith in public life.

At the other end of the spectrum there are still countries where State taxes finance the Church. In Denmark, Norway, Sweden and Finland the Lutheran Church is paid for by public taxation. Switzerland pays its ministers through taxes though people can opt out and give to a charity fund (as in Germany). To the Swiss (like Chalmers) the concept of voluntary giving means dependence on the bourgeois.

In yet other countries the established religion is one which has proved to be an intolerant and persecuting faith. This is true, to varying degrees, of all Muslim countries (it is interesting that many Muslims would demand civil rights in this country which most Muslim countries would not even contemplate for Christians) and of some Roman Catholic countries. The Presbyterians in Mexico and evangelicals in some other countries have and still are experiencing this type of intolerance – where all evangelicals are cast as cults and treated accordingly by their governments. It is interesting that in a country like Peru the power of the Roman Church has been considerably weakened as its links with the State have been weakened – and as freedom has been granted to more and more outside the Church. Evangelicals are now playing an increasingly important role in government and are having to face up to the implications of Church–State relations.

In Britain, where the Church is in decline, the question of the establishment of the Church of England is one that is likely to raise its head again in the coming years. The Church of England, whilst being the established Church, has a membership which is only 8% of the population. Within Britain at the moment it would be extremely foolish to call the country a Christian nation when only a fraction of the population even attend any kind of Church. Despite that the fact remains that, as Mrs. Thatcher recognised, 'the Christian religion is a fundamental part of our national heritage ... indeed we are a nation whose ideals are founded on the Bible' (Margaret Thatcher, Text of Speech to Church of Scotland General Assembly, p.27). So how does the establishment affect this nation where the national Church is in a state of decline and disarray? How can it be applied to Scotland where the Church is stronger but where the trend is still downwards? What relationships should we be looking for between the Church of Scotland and the State? What is our vision for the future?

THE DUTY OF THE STATE TO THE CHURCH

'Society ought to be an institution of good, not of mere punishment – not of mere negative protection' (Pamphlet, *New Testament Sanction of the National Establishment and Spiritual Liberty of the Church of Christ*, p.12).

According to Calvin it is the duty of the State to ensure that 'men breathe, eat, drink and are kept warm' (Calvin, quoted in Keddie, *op. cit.*, p.25). However we are concerned not with the general responsibilities of the State but with the State's duty as regards the Church. It is the duty of the State to provide circumstances so that 'we may live peaceful and quiet lives in all godliness and holiness' (1 Timothy 2.2). It is also the duty of the State to support and encourage Biblical Christianity. There are several ways that this could be done, even in a multi-cultural society like ours. The first is that the State could provide financial and material support for the Church. To some extent the State already does this. The current Free Church would be in a desperate state financially if it were not for deeds of covenant, by which we are able to claim on taxes that our members pay to the State. We also accept grants from State-funded bodies such as the Historic Buildings Council and rates concessions because we are a State-recognised charity.

There should be no embarrassment in the Free Church when a new congregation, (as happened with Smithton-Culloden near Inverness), applies for aid from the local Council for building a church. The building is after all a community asset and if local councils can offer money to do up derelict castles they can give money to provide churches. If the Council tried to lay down conditions which were unacceptable to the Church (ie dictated the times and content of the services) then the Church would just forget about a grant. Equally the Council are under no obligation to give money and they must consider whether the church will be a service to the local community.

Looking to the future, if there were to be a revival of Biblical Christianity, we might perhaps look for a system of State grants on the Swiss line, whereby individuals who did not want to pay a Church tax could opt to allow their money to go to a charity of their choice. This is similar to the Trade Union levy imposed on its members for the Labour party. If they feel strongly about it they can opt out. An individual could designate the Church or charity that his tax was to go to. Only recognised Churches would be eligible to receive the moneys concerned. Those organisations which were anti-Christian or cults would be tolerated but not allowed any State support. This may seem somewhat utopian but it must be remembered that we are looking at a time when the Gospel will have greatly prospered and it is also the experience of other countries.

The State could also fund the Church in her social work. Again to some extent this is already done – the £13 million budget of the Church of Scotland Social Work Department is to a large extent funded by the State. One encouraging sign in British politics recently has been the emphasis on wider choice in education. As the State funds what has now become education in secular humanism, what is to stop it funding those schools which would want to be specifically Christian? Perhaps it could be along the line of the Dutch model where if 50 families get together the State will finance the school without dictating every aspect of the curriculum. The State sees that certain conditions are complied with – ie teacher/pupil ratios, proper use of buildings, teacher qualifications, curriculum design. Historically education and the Church have always been linked in Scotland. Until 1861 teachers in Scotland had to hold to the teaching of the Westminster Confession and schools were subject to inspection by the Presbytery. When in 1872 the Church in Scotland lost control of its schools to the State, I am sure that it did not anticipate that it would lead to the situation we have today where in many of our schools our children are being taught to disbelieve in the God of the Bible! It is somewhat ironic that in Scotland today, the country where there was the most thorough Reformation, it is only Roman Catholic schools that receive State funding (although the Labour party is currently proposing that there could be State funded Muslim schools!). The dissatisfaction that is caused by this could be alleviated if other Christian groups were allowed the opportunity to receive State funding.

In other areas such as broadcasting, housing, medicine and social work, there could also be more co-operation between State and Church. The limitations on Christian broadcasting are a limitation of our freedom. In a so-called Christian country, to allow a pornographer to own and run a TV station, and to refuse a Church is somewhat ludicrous. There is already a good measure of co-operation in some areas between the National Health Service and the Church. Hospital chaplains are a religious service provided by the Church. But as the NHS and medicine in general moves towards a holistic approach involving mind and emotion as well as body – is it too much to ask that spiritual wellbeing be taken more into consideration? And if there is a revival of true Christianity then we will hopefully see a reversal of the current demise of medical ethics. The State deciding that a human being is not really a human being and does not have the right to live, as has happened in Britain with the issue of abortion, is a State which has gone well beyond its authority and has taken to itself the role of God.

Yet another duty of the State is to ensure that there is a measure of liberty and toleration of other views. Christianity must never seek to impose itself upon people by force. Chalmers' argument for a Protestant establishment was radical in that it also argued for toleration of Roman Catholics and Catholic emancipation. Today we must emphasise over and over again that we have no desire to engage in persecuting principles. The Confession of Faith, chapter 23, would seem to allow for the State to use force to compel people to believe (at least, that is what the English Parliament thought at the time) but the Free Church amended or explained it so that it specifically disavowed persecuting principles. There must continue to be an absolute guarantee of rights for the non-believer. This does not mean that there will be a total free-for-all in the name of religion where any one can start up a religion and claim State support. In a State where Biblical Christianity is the established religion there will be toleration, but no support for, those of other viewpoints. An example of this is a debate that took place in the Edinburgh University Students' Association a number of years ago. On the one side were those who argued that in the name of 'free-speech' the Moonies should be given access to Association funds and Union buildings on the same basis as other religious bodies. On the other side there were those who argued that the Association had a policy of not allowing fascist speakers (the Moonies were notoriously right-wing), that the Moonies engaged in brain-washing and that this would be a misuse of Association funds. The latter point of view won the day. This did not mean that Moonies were not allowed to be students, nor to propagate their views. It did mean that they would not receive any help in so doing. In a Christian country non-Christian religions would receive no State support whereas Christians would. This would mean that there would be no State-aided Muslim schools or Mosques but that freedom would be granted to Muslims.

It is also the duty of the State not to interfere in the internal affairs of the Church. As the State had no right to tell the people in Scotland what ministers to choose, so it has no right to allow the Prime Minister or the Queen to appoint bishops. The head of the State may be the Queen – but the head of the Church is Jesus Christ. One example of undue State interference in the Church has been the attempt in recent years by some MPs to introduce legislation through Parliament, to enforce the ordination of women in the Church of England. It is possible that a government might decide that a Church which was being Biblical by not allowing the ordination of women was breaking the law. The Church would then have to continue to break that law, as the government has no right to make the Church go against the Word of God.

The State does not exist to give pleasure and self glory to individuals; it does not exist for the benefit of a king or ruling class and it does not exist for its own glory (the wrong kind of nationalism). It exists ultimately to bring glory to God and it only does so as it applies the basic principles of the Word to itself. Peace, prosperity, justice and true freedom are the foundation aims of a State which could truly be called Christian.

In summary the duty of the State as regards the Church is to support the work of the Gospel by creating favourable conditions for the Church. We do not argue for one particular denomination in Britain at this time to be given sole recognition – as none has the support of anything like a majority. Nor do we argue that there is no place in Britain for those of other faiths. They just would not receive any State support. Nor would every Church have to be registered. Those who did not agree with the principle of the State supporting the Church would be free to go it on their own. However we do feel that it is right that a national recognition be made of the Christian faith and that that recognition remain a Protestant one. This will bring great benefits to the State as was recognised in that remarkable speech by Margaret Thatcher to the General Assembly of the Church of Scotland on 21 May 1988 – 'Your success matters greatly – as much to the temporal as to the spiritual welfare of the nation' (Margaret Thatcher, *op. cit.*, p. 40).

THE DUTY OF THE CHURCH TO THE STATE

'We cannot abandon politics to those who carry guns, or for that matter to those who carry pocket calculators' (N.T. Wright, *The New Testament and the State*, p.16).

The Church has a duty to the State, whether it is recognised by the State or not. Our duty is first of all to pray for 'kings and those in authority, that we may live peaceful and quiet lives in all godliness' (1 Timothy 2.2). The Church must never forget this responsibility and never underestimate the power of prayer in national events. The second main element of the Bible's teaching is that we must obey the law of the land and teach all Christians to do likewise. The only time that we may disobey is when the law of the land opposes the law of God. We have no right to disobey the law just because we do not like it.

However, the Church's responsibility to the State goes beyond obedience to the law of the land. We have to proclaim the law of God to the State so that the State governs in accordance with Biblical principles. Like the prophets of the Old Testament, the prophetic people of God in the New must call nations, politicians, rulers and those in authority to repentance. 'Now listen you rich people, weep and wail because of the misery that is coming upon you ... Look! The wages you failed to pay the workmen who mowed your fields are crying out against you. The cries of the harvesters have reached the ears of the Lord Almighty' (James 5.1–5). The Church must act as the conscience of the nation. And so we have a right and a duty to speak about those issues where there are clear guidelines in the Word of God. That does not mean that we have the right to tell the government the details of its economic and social policies – but we can give them the principles within which they ought to work. As a Church we cannot say whether the level of income tax should be ten, twenty or thirty pence in the pound. But what we can say is that the principle of justice would require a government to ensure that taxation was fair and geared towards ability to pay.

The Church fails in its task if it preaches a social Gospel that is nothing more than religious socialism, conservatism, liberalism or nationalism. But it equally fails if it does not spell out the implications of God's Word for the society we live in. The Free Church of Scotland today, like many other churches, may feel free and duty bound to speak out about Sunday ferries and sexual immorality. We must also feel free to address ourselves to the injustice and unrighteousness in every area in our society. To do so is the best way to follow the example of our forefathers.

Going hand in hand with the application of Biblical principles to the society we live in, must come the proclamation of the Gospel. As Mrs. Thatcher reminded the Church of Scotland 'there is little hope for democracy if the hearts of men and women in democratic societies cannot be touched by a call to something greater than themselves. Political structures, State institutions, collective ideals are not enough. We parliamentarians can legislate for the rule of law. You, the Church, can teach the life of faith' (Margaret Thatcher, *op. cit.*, p.36). It is impossible to have a just society without just people. It is impossible to have a changed society without changed people. Therefore all the social work and political involvement in the world will not change the injustice in the world, unless there is a revival of true Christianity in the land. We preach the Gospel and we preach its implications to all of society. In Biblical Christianity there can be no place for a selfish individualism, nor for a political utopianism.

Should we have Christian political parties? This is a difficult question but my inclination would be to say 'no' because there is not a specific Christian political policy. If there were a Christian political party it would have to make decisions about such issues as Scottish independence, housing policy, income tax levels, etc. It then runs the danger of turning away from the Gospel those people who do not support the particular stance taken, as Christianity then becomes identified with a particular policy. Christians should work within the existing political structures if at all possible. However if, as seems likely, the current political parties remove themselves further and further from Biblical morality it may mean that a party with a distinctive Christian ethos should be set up. It is a sad fact that the unjust electoral system in our country would militate against such a move being successful. If there was a system of proportional representation then it would be possible to have a specifically Christian representation in Parliament.

Should ministers be involved in politics? The answer must be yes and no! Ministers, who are paid to give themselves to the full-time ministry of the Word and pastoral work, if they are doing their job properly do not have the time to be Councillors or MPs. That work should generally be left to others called by God. What ministers can do is spell out the practical implications of the faith and encourage others to get more involved. There is a desperate need for Christians to be involved in politics, at every level and in every party.

There is one further aspect of the duty of the Church to society that was vital to the Disruption fathers and must be vital to us – education. We must urgently look at the possibility of setting up Christian schools. As the government has moved to a more centralised control of education – and as schools take it upon themselves to teach sex education, religion, evolution, politics and social skills, as well as reinterpreting our history, surely there will come a point when we must say enough is enough. And then what will happen? Will middle-class Christian children be sent to private Christian schools, and the rest of society left to rot under the influence of secular humanism? Or will we have enough vision to establish schools which will be open to all who desire an education based on Christian principles? We should be prepared to put our beliefs about the establishment principle into practice and seek government funding for education. At the moment in some areas the need does not appear to be that great because of the linkage between Church, school and individual Christian teachers and families. But the situation is not improving and the Church must be ready.

There is much then that the Church has to do in its relationship with the State. We should be thankful for the residue of Christianity that remains in the national institutions of Scotland. And we should seek to play an active and positive role in the development of our society, as long as we are able to. Salt and light is perhaps the best motto of all!

CONCLUSION

'Certainly we do not want men to allow their Christianity to flow over into their political life, for the establishment of anything like a really just society would be major disaster' (Screwtape in *Screwtape Letters*, quoted by Arthur Simon, *Christian Faith and Public Policy. No Grounds for Divorce*, p.83).

Our Spanish brethren, whom we read about at the beginning, were wrong to refuse the money offered to them by the State. They could have taken the money with good conscience and used it to the glory of God. But at least they were consistent to their view of strict separation between Church and State. Perhaps the majority of evangelicals would hold to that view in theory – but I wonder how many are prepared to give up deeds of covenant and government grants?

As we have seen there is an undoubted Biblical connection between the Church and the State. In an ideal situation the Church would be united and pure and the State would be just. Because there is not such an ideal in existence does that mean that we should not work for it? (Christians after all are to strive to be perfect although none of us attain that state this side of glory!) There are many more things that we could look at in this important subject, but let it suffice to say that if we want to be true to the principles of our forefathers, and more importantly to the teaching of Scripture, we must widen our vision, open our mouths and work with our hands, for a just and peaceful society in which the Gospel is freely proclaimed to all men and people are able to live 'peaceful and quiet lives in all godliness and holiness. This is good and pleases God our Saviour, who wants all men to be saved and to come to a knowledge of the truth' (1 Timothy 2.2).

The Church of 1843 looked to the day when God 'in his own good time, will restore to them these benefits (of an established free Church), the fruits of the struggles and sufferings of their fathers in times past in the same cause; and thereafter, give them grace to employ them more effectually than hitherto they have done for the manifestation of his glory' (Free Church Blue Book, p.116). In other words they looked for a time when the relationship between Church and State would be restored and when true Biblical Christianity, and a truly free Church would be recognised and supported by the State.

Today, although that prospect may seem remote, the Free Church should continue to call for Biblical principles to be put into practice, at every level of Government; whether it is local, national or international. We should also expect the State, whether the British State or a separate Scottish State, to recognise and support the Christian faith. A revitalised Christian Scotland (or Britain or Europe!) may seem unlikely at the present time, humanly speaking. But we are not speaking in human terms alone. God is able, and as we continue to proclaim the Gospel we must have the vision and expectation that the Gospel will prosper and have impact, not only on individuals, but also on our society.

3

Worship: The Heart of Religion

HECTOR CAMERON

THE PLACE OF WORSHIP

Christians are not required to suppress their feelings of attachment for their place of worship, least of all their ancestral place of worship. In this most literal of senses God's servants take pleasure in the stones of Zion. Along with other Presbyterians at the same time, we in the Free Church see it as important to affirm our belief that 'neither prayer, nor any other part of religious worship is, now under the Gospel, either tied unto, or made more acceptable by any place in which it is performed, or towards which it is directed; but God is to be worshipped everywhere in spirit and in truth: as in private families daily, and in secret each one by himself: so more solemnly in the public assemblies'. The early Christian Church both believed this and practised it. The Jewish temple with its priestly associations had reached its Gospel terminus with the coming of Christ. A dwelling-house or some open air site was as good a place as any for a Church meeting, when other venues failed.

Of course as time went by special church buildings were built. That, however, was a gesture to convenience and not to better spirituality. It was only as the religious life of the Church suffered a certain weakening or decay in one place or another that church buildings began to be looked on as sanctuaries and reverenced as sacred. This New Testament doctrine that the place of worship does not really matter and that God's presence is assured His people wherever His name is invoked, must have meant much to our Covenanting and Disruption forefathers, who many times were driven to the fields and hills for public worship. It is equally welcome at a time when old church buildings may have to be replaced on the score of wear and tear, and churches put up in entirely new places in the course of Gospel outreach. The blessings we associate with our church do not come or go with the building.

CHARACTERISTICS OF CHRISTIAN WORSHIP

Our Confession of Faith traces the origins of religious worship to where man encounters the revelation, brought him by 'the light of nature', that there is a God who has lordship and sovereignty over all, and who both is good and does good unto all. He is for these reasons to be 'feared, loved, praised, called upon, trusted in and served, with all the heart, and with all the soul, and with all the might'. The force of this for our worship of God at all stages deserves to be underlined. Any loss of regard either for the absolute greatness of God, or for his absolute goodness, is bound to disable and disfigure our worship, to say no more. Meanwhile, we do still possess certain instincts, fumbling instincts they may be, in the direction of acknowledging our Maker. Sin, however, having depraved our moral nature and violated our relations with God, has left us bereft, since the Fall, of any true understanding of the worship of God. The Confession goes on therefore to say that 'the acceptable way of worshipping the true God is instituted by himself, and is so limited by his own revealed will that he may not be worshipped according to the imaginations and devices of men, or the suggestions of Satan, under any visible representation, or any other way not prescribed in the Holy Scriptures'.

Attention is then at once directed to the two great distinguishing features of Christian worship – and the two around which serious error most readily tends to gather – namely that it is Trinitarian and that it is Evangelical. 'Religious worship is to be given to God, the Father, Son and Holy Ghost, and to him alone, and since the fall, not without a mediator, nor the mediation of any other but of Christ alone.'

These teachings are specially relevant for our own day and age. We live at a time when unitarianism, both within the Christian Church and outside it, is on the march. No age was ever in more urgent need of the Christian doctrine of the Trinity, especially where the developed doctrine of the love of the Father, the grace of the Son, and the fellowship of the Spirit brings assurance of every conceivable blessing to the Church. With that doctrine the Unitarian faith stands in bleak and comfortless opposition. Nor did any generation ever require more urgently the central Gospel message of Christ our Mediator: not simply, it has to be said, because in the absence of that message the world must perish without God, but because today large sections of the Christian Church who undertake to proclaim God to their fellow men have all but lost the Gospel which tells men how to reach him.

Having established the position that no worship is acceptable to God unless it is prescribed in the holy Scripture, the authors of our Confession (commonly referred to as the Westminster Divines) proceed to list six 'parts' or divisions belonging to public worship – prayer, the reading of the Word, sound preaching of the Word, conscionable listening to it, the singing of Psalms and the administration of the sacraments – by divine appointment. In connection with these a number of topics of special interest for our subject may be picked out.

THE PRIORITY OF THE WORD IN WORSHIP

It is our belief as Presbyterians that what we call 'extraordinary' channels of revelation formerly employed to convey God's will to men, channels such as prophets and apostles, have for ever ceased. The better to preserve and propagate the truth which God has communicated to His Church 'at sundry times and in diverse manners' in history, He has committed it entirely to writing, which the Church now possesses in the shape of the Old and New Testament Scriptures. To this, says our Confession, 'nothing is to be added at any time, whether by new revelations of the Spirit or traditions of men'.

The Divines were thinking at this point of (1) the emergence from time to time on the periphery of the Church of various sects claiming to have received heavenly messages which were to be placed on a level with the Bible; in practice above it. Their distinctive error lay in substituting the Spirit, or what they took to be the Spirit, for the Word of God; and (2) the ecclesiastical dogmas of the Church of Rome, which sees the need for a supplement to the Bible and claims to have found such a supplement in the way of fifteen or so apocryphal books, the vast theological output of the Greek and Latin Fathers, and a great collection of Church Council deliverances and papal edicts. Rome and the sects have corrupted the teaching of the Bible and have in places virtually cancelled it out for their constituencies.

Christians in the Reformed tradition, as the Westminster Confession makes plain, have given to the Word of God a particular place of honour in their lives and church services. They view the Word as the only rule of faith and obedience. The Word, read or preached, and blessed by God's Spirit, becomes an effectual means of convincing and converting sinners and thereafter of sanctifying them. It is the tribunal before which religious controversies must be resolved, Church decrees examined and the 'opinions of ancient writers, doctrines of men and private spirits' assessed. The Word also regulates the worship of the Church, as we have seen, on the principle that nothing should be introduced into the worship of God unless it is prescribed in Scripture. Texts referred to include Deuteronomy 12:32, 'What thing soever I command you, observe to do it', and Matthew, 15:9, 'In vain do they worship me, teaching for doctrines the commandments of men'.

To give to the Word such a status has practical implications for the style of religious service to be expected from churches which concur. Presbyterians tend to be viewed as dour and their services dull. There may well be Presbyterians who approximate to that description. Usually, however, the criticism has been prompted by the plainness of the church buildings, the subdued complexion of the services, the strictly basic character of the ritual, the conspicuous lack of activity up at the front (apart from the preacher) or the less than picturesque attire of the church officials.

The fact is that the very real contrast between the typical presbyterian service of worship and those of many other churches is something substantially due to the Word of God; or rather to the role which presbyterianism considers the Word of God to deserve. The Word of God regulates for them the worship of God. That, of course, might be confessed by virtually all Christian churches – not excluding the Church of Rome. The question then is, In what sense or to what extent does the Word of God regulate the worship of God? It is when the ultimate step is taken, which the Westminster Divines as disciples of John Calvin did take, to the point where they say, 'If the thing is prescribed by the Word of God, fine, if not, we must exclude it,' that is when the parting of the ways is reached.

At the furthest remove from the Westminster position is that of the Roman Catholic Church. Cardinal Bellarmine, a 16th/17th century theologian, indicates the basic teaching of his Church on the subject of authority: 'We assert that all necessary doctrine concerning faith and morals is not expressly contained in Scripture, and consequently, besides the written Word, there is needed an unwritten one; whereas they (the Reformers) teach that in the Scriptures all such necessary doctrine is contained'. Incidentally it should be noted that the Reformers as a whole, like the Westminster

Divines following in their footsteps, in fact taught that all necessary doctrine 'is either expressly set down in Scripture, or by good and necessary consequence may be deduced from Scripture'. Meanwhile, the degree of freedom which the Church of Rome sees her own principle of authority as conferring may be judged from the presence of priests in the services who are deemed to have a mediatorial role, the invocation of saints and the veneration of Mary, and the celebration of the Mass as 'a true and proper propitiatory sacrifice'.

Lying mid-way between the Roman and Reformed (at any rate Calvinist) views on how far worship is to be regulated by the Word, is the position held by the Lutheran and Anglican Reformers. Here the Church is seen as having a certain authority to introduce rites and ceremonies into public worship. This may be done, however, only if these observances are not forbidden in the Word of God (cf. Art. 20, Church of England). This view, while it confines within given limits the Church's freedom to create new worship observances, is clearly a good deal less restrictive (or more loose!) than Calvin's. The thing to do is search the Word of God with a particular fresh ingredient for the Church's programme of worship in mind, and if you nowhere see the Word prohibiting such a step you go ahead. Calvin, like his Puritan and Presbyterian successors, on the other hand, looked for a positive warrant in the Word for each religious observance included in the Church's worship.

PULPIT AND COMMUNION TABLE

One of the ways in which the Presbyterian service will differ more or less strikingly from the Roman – and in many instances Anglican – form of worship can be sensed from the very geography of the building. The Presbyterian pulpit occupies a robustly central stance at the front of the church. It is true that there are Presbyterian churches where the pulpit has moved away to one side, and it is the communion table at the far and front end of the building, as in Anglican and Roman churches, which catches the worshipper's eye. This may not in given cases conflict seriously with the Gospel. It is not on the other hand Presbyterian, and cannot but serve, in other cases, as a distraction from the Presbyterian insistence on the centrality of the Word.

Traditionally in Presbyterian churches, the communion table was not represented at all in the pulpit or lectern area of the church.

The post-Reformation Scots did indeed want a distinct communion table in their churches, and their Commissioners held considerable debate with the English Independents at the Westminster Assembly on this precise question. The Independents, by and large, preferred to observe the communion with minimum ceremony, using the ordinary pews. The Scots, it is on record, considered this practice to be bare to the point of irreverence! Many Scottish churches in former days did some ingenious carpentry work on some of the front centre seats, to allow the rapid deployment of long tables around which the communicants sat (thus assisting the symbolism of the Christian family table) and to allow the equally rapid return of things to normal (presumably lest the symbolism should get out of hand in a Romeward way by becoming a fixture). Interestingly, the Act of the Scottish General Assembly adopting the Directory for Public Worship indicates that the main reason for having the communicants seated around the table was to permit them to serve themselves, rather than be served individually by the minister, whose part it was merely to 'begin the action'. The alternative would have been too reminiscent of priestly pre-Reformation days and was probably not without its real dangers.

All of this was agreeable with the spirit of the Directory where it says, 'Let all enter the assembly (church meeting) in a grave and seemly manner, taking their seats or places without adoration or bowing themselves towards one place or another'. It was being insisted on (a) that the Word should hold first place in worship, relative to the sacraments most particularly; (b) that any hint of the communion being observed under anything like priestly auspices, or as an ordinance bringing automatic benefits, was out of keeping with the Gospel; and (c) that it was much easier than people believed to slip into a veneration of earthly persons and things which conflicted with the exclusive worship prerogatives of God.

PULPIT VERSUS AUDIENCE PARTICIPATION

Onwards from the Reformation the 'preliminaries' of Protestant services (singing, reading and prayer) had been conducted by a non-ministerial 'reader'. Indeed the minister as often as not entered the church only when due to go to the pulpit to preach, at which point he himself would assume charge of the service. The Westminster Assembly, much against the wishes of the Scots Commissioners in fact, excluded the office of reader from their Directory.

The Directory states that the duty of reading the Word is to be performed by the minister, although occasionally, with consent of Presbytery, by a divinity student. However, it can be seen that when Presbyterianism was given its definitive form, there were only slight points of disagreement over the sharing of leadership roles in public worship. By common consent, no more than one or two men, duly licensed to read and preach, together with the leader of praise, (often the minister), figured in any prominent way in the service.

Aside from a minor difference of viewpoint here and there, that is the way things still stand, wherever the Presbyterian conception of worship is taken seriously. There is of course the main body of worshippers, in whose name the minister leads the prayers, and leads also (or nowadays most often his deputy does) the joint praise, and for whose edification he is appointed to read and expound the Word, and dispense the sacraments. This accords with the Reformation dictum that the ministry is for the sake of the Church, and not the other way round (Philippians 2:17). In any event wider leadership arrangements are seen neither to be needed nor valid for the normal service of worship. Among exceptional situations would be the Communion service where ruling elders assist the minister in distributing the bread and wine.

Visitors from other churches today would probably find the Presbyterian form of worship on the staid side. Increasingly, with the development of charismatic styles of worship, there is a desire for something like audience participation in the services of the Church, and Church leaders are often not unwilling to comply. Biblical support is claimed for the practice. The Corinthian Church, instead of being seen as representing an early stage in the establishment of Christianity, and as a Church besides where many of the canons of apostolic teaching and practice were being transgressed, is taken to represent the model Church service scene, normative for today.

Mainline Presbyterian theology has continued fairly constant in its views upon this question. Dr. James Bannerman, a leading Disruption Church theologian, sees the simple service of worship, led by a minister, as the ultimate form of Christian public worship, established by the apostles of Christ in their teaching and already taking practical shape during their lifetime. Around the apostles in the process were gathered the great variety of charismatic gifts and functionaries, whose role was to assist the apostles (who were themselves outstandingly endowed with miracle powers) with the transition from Old Testament Church worship. These, says Bannerman, 'formed no part of the ordinary equipment of the Church of Christ or the ordinary staff of office-bearers by which its affairs were to be administered. Their use and function ceased when the Church of Christ through their instrumentality had been finally settled and fully organised, and when it had attained to the condition of its ordinary and permanent development' (*The Church of Christ*, vol. 1, pp. 215–16).

This temporary charismatic organisation, which was necessary at a time when the Christian Church had not as yet been established, has often been appealed to, Bannerman notes, as the 'rule and model for the proper and permanent condition of society'. For Bannerman this involves a serious misreading of Scripture. The charismatic gifts, having served their purpose of ministering to the arrival of New Testament revelation and the final organisation of Christ's Church, were to cease. The Scripture quoted in support of the Confession of Faith's assertion that 'these former ways of God's revealing His will unto His people are now ceased' is Hebrews chapter 2. This chapter looks back from the time when it was written to the experience of former days when God had borne witness to Christ 'with signs and wonders and with diverse miracles and gifts of the Holy Ghost, according to His will'. And although the immediate experience in question belonged to the Hebrews to whom the epistle was penned, there are, when the New Testament at large is taken into account, wider implications. Such miraculous testimonies, occurring early in the life of the Church but sooner or later passing away, were remembered as a general and not as an isolated experience.

PRAISE

When the Divines state in the 21st chapter of the Confession that the 'singing of Psalms with grace in the heart' is to be part of the worship of God, they meant psalms, beyond doubt, in the precise sense of the Book of Psalms. Their *Directory for Public Worship*, published a year or two earlier, exhorted congregations to sing psalms and that people who could read should acquire a psalm book. This straightforward request addressed to uncomplicated people was never likely to be misunderstood. As part of the same operation, also, the Divines had recommended Rouse's version of the metrical psalms for use throughout the three kingdoms. Instrumental music meantime, in keeping with the firm views of the Second Reformation men as a class, was never raised. It has to be assumed, at the same time, that the Divines regarded their instructions about the praise side of public worship as resting very comfortably on their fundamental worship principle, that only what the Word prescribes can become part of the worship of God; as comfortably as did prayer, the reading and preaching of the Word, and the administration of the sacraments.

THE DISRUPTION CHURCH AND THE DEBATE ABOUT PRAISE

The Westminster Divines have given us, in their Confession and Catechisms, a set of statements about worship which Presbyterians see as distilling the best of Reformed conclusions bearing on the fundamental principles at issue. It is, however, to the Disruption men we must turn for the most wide-ranging and thorough development of these principles on the central topics involved. The first generation of Disruption Church leaders were occupied, almost to the exclusion of anything else, with great questions concerning the freedom of the Church from State control, and the whole Church was of course exhausted with its incessant labours during that period. Nevertheless there was provided a valuable legacy for their successors in the way of profound, sustained and accurate thinking from a Biblical base, on a number of extremely difficult subjects. It was an advantage too for the developing theology of Church praise that the Church should have been flung into the most animated of debates on the psalms/hymns question by reason of the negotiations for union with the hymn-singing United Presbyterian Church. The point is that there was nothing sterile about the arguments entered into. Even if, as nearly always happens in the party-forming turmoil of theological debate, the politics of winning the day for one's position could not be excluded, there took place a great deal of able, inspired and learned Biblical discussion around the issues raised. A brief reference to one or two salient features of this debate may not be out of place.

Wide Range of Views

What strikes one first of all in a Church united in a quite remarkable way so recently on the Disruption issue, is the variety of approaches which figured in the debates about praise. The whole range was there, from knowledgeable defenders of the classical Presbyterian position on Psalmody, to participants who, for whatever reason, were intent on tackling the issue from scratch, as if the Westminster documents had nothing material to say. There were men who thought in terms of the peace of the Church, men who regarded union with other church bodies as the paramount issue, and men who believed that the divisions over worship which seemed to threaten Church union, could be resolved in the new uniting Church by the open question method; allowing each congregation in the new Church to practice their own convictions about worship. Somewhere in the middle there were men like Dr. Robert Candlish. Candlish vigorously maintained that the regulative Principle of worship excluded instrumental music from Christian worship (otherwise the Church returned to the Jewish Temple) and yet claimed a New Testament liberty to introduce hymns.

Theological Defences of Presbyterian Worship

There was a remarkable degree of theological opposition to musical instruments in worship, among Disruption men, as distinct from a merely traditional conviction that the old way of things was better. This was partly due, there can be no question, to the publication by Dr. Candlish in 1856 of Dr. Porteous's able defence – in the name of the Glasgow Presbytery – of the Reformed objection to instrumental music in worship. Dr. Porteous was replying to the action of the St. Andrew's Congregation in Glasgow, who had in 1807, without even consulting Presbytery, installed an organ in their church. Candlish's warm introductory commendation of the book sent it on its way with superbly attractive credentials, especially for the emerging generation of Free Churchmen.

Porteous drew substantially on the views of the Reformers, although he conducted a wider and very informative historical study of the subject. Luther is quoted as exclaiming that 'organs are among the ensigns of Baal'! Calvin's opinions are extensively consulted. For example, 'Instrumental music is not fitter to be adopted into the public worship of the Christian Church than the incense, the candlesticks and the other shadows of the Mosaic law ... Instrumental music we therefore maintain was only tolerated on account of the times and of the people, because they were as boys, as the sacred Scripture speaketh, whose condition required these puerile rudiments. But in Gospel times we must not have recourse to these, unless we wish to destroy the evangelical perfection, and to obscure the meridian light which we enjoy in Christ our Lord'. The younger Disruption men were directed back to their origins with undoubtedly good effect.

Dr. Cunningham and the Force of the Regulative Principle

It is a matter of regret that Dr. William Cunningham, easily the most accomplished theologian of his era, seems to have written nothing, certainly not in his published works, bearing directly on the subject of psalms versus hymns. Cunningham's day was in fact already far spent by the time that any serious debate on the subject had got under way in the Free Church. He died in 1861, and the first formal step to seek union with the United Presbyterian Church, a hymn-singing body, was not taken until the Free Church Assembly of 1863.

We do fortunately have some account of his views on the question of instrumental music in worship. Cunningham follows the Reformation men closely in his theological scrutiny of the issues, but injects his own characteristic treatment of things into the debate. It must have pained lovers of church music to find the worthy Doctor referring to organs as 'ineptiae', 'small matters' and 'paltry stuff'! These were his very words. Taken by themselves such epithets might suggest that Cunningham was merely expressing some personal revulsion towards instrumental music in church, much as he would have done about an undesirable item of food. This is far from being the case. The 'paltry stuff' concerned – to which class of things in Cunningham's view church organs belonged – was for him out of place in public worship, not from the point of view of being a nuisance but as conflicting with a certain great Biblical principle.

This is what he says: 'There is a strange fallacy which seems to mislead men in forming an estimate of the soundness and importance of this principle (the regulative principle). Because this principle has been often brought out in connection with the discussion of matters which, viewed in themselves are very unimportant, such as rites and ceremonies, vestments and organs, crossings, kneeling and bowing, and other such "ineptiae", some men seem to think that it partakes of the intrinsic littleness of these things, and that the men who defend it and try to enforce it find their most congenial occupation in fighting about these matters, and exhibit great bigotry and narrow-mindedness in bringing the authority of God and the testimony of Scripture to bear upon such a number of petty points'.

The regulative principle, as such, Cunningham goes on to say, is taught with sufficient plainness in Scripture, and is itself 'large, liberal and comprehensive'. If there were signs of smallness around, this was not due to the principle inherently, nor its supporters, but 'to the conduct of the men who in defiance of this principle would obtrude human inventions into the worship of the Church, or insist upon retaining them when they are admitted. It is enough for us that they (the human inventions) have no positive sanction from Scripture. On this ground we refuse to admit them, and where they have crept in, we insist upon them being turned out, although upon this latter point, Calvin, with his usual magnanimity, was always willing to have a reasonable regard to times and circumstances, and to the weakness and infirmities of the parties concerned'. He sums up his argument thus: 'All we have to do with the mass of trumpery that has been brought under discussion in connection with these subjects . . . is to apply this principle to the mass of paltry stuff that has been devised for improving and adorning the Church and thereby we sweep it all away'. Stirring words! Yes, certainly, but words which effectively delivered the regulative principle from one of the most serious misrepresentations directed against it up till that time.

An Ordinance of Song

The Disruption Church defenders of the position that only 'inspired materials of praise' could be used in public worship were at one in seeing the Biblical text itself as the necessary basis of the songs it was proper to sing. Some holding this view would almost certainly have understood the term to include paraphrases – in the popular sense of passages of Scripture not originally in the form of songs but which have been given a metrical structure. But supporters of the traditional presbyterian position in the main fell into two groups: (1) Those who took the expression 'inspired materials of praise' to refer simply to the Book of Psalms, and (2) those who differed from them to the point of being prepared to include other Biblical songs of praise than those found in the Book of Psalms (eg the two songs of Moses), or who had a still open mind on such songs. Dr. James Begg was one of the latter. He was a steadfast defender of the Book of

Psalms as against uninspired hymns, but had not as yet conclusively decided against 'similarly constructed and equally inspired materials which the Bible affords' as due a place in the Church's worship.

Principles of Psalm Selection in the Old Testament

One of the best recent studies on whether to supplement the Book of Psalms from other Old Testament songs occurs as part of a wider study by the late Major W.M. Mackay, Dundee (Captain Good Hope to erstwhile readers of *The Instructor*). His article 'The Praise of the Sanctuary', was published in *The Monthly Record* of April 1956. Major Mackay's leading thought is that the Book of Psalms is uniquely suitable to be the Church's book of praise. Taking up the sub-theme 'Principles of Psalm Selection' he indicates that one of the principles followed in the preparation of the Book of Psalms was that only songs suitable for use in praise by all people are included. That does not exclude reference to Jewish matters, he says, since the Jewish economy was a typical one; it prefigured Christ, and its history brings out God's purpose and government in a way which is basic for the Christian dispensation.

On the other hand the Psalms were not intended merely or primarily as a Jewish praise book. Had they been so intended, the two songs of Moses could not possibly have been omitted. Although the song of Exodus 15 is not included as a whole, seven Psalms refer to the dividing of the sea, and eighteen contain passages parallel to Deuteronomy 32. The Song of Deborah is of significance mainly for Israel, and is excluded, but a phrase of it – 'Lead thy captivity captive' – appears in Psalm 68. The Song of Hannah is excluded, but one portion of it is reproduced in Psalm 113:7–8, and every verse of it is quoted elsewhere. David's lament for Jonathan is not included – it is not praise of God – and appears to be one of the merely human and uninspired utterances of David. David's last words are not included, although inspired, being personal to himself. 'We conclude, then', Major Mackay sums up, 'that songs which were truly national songs of Israel were not included, but only such as were in a form suitable to be the substance of praise to God for wider use, and by other nations.'

A Divinely Ordained Book of Song

The main line of defence in favour of Psalms adopted by the Disruption men laid stress on a divinely given ordinance of song. And there was, they pointed out, a divinely ordained book of song to go with it. This was their particular form of reply to men like Candlish and Arnot, who argued that the Book of Psalms was as much a book of prayer as it was a book of praise. If the Book of Psalms was a book of prayer, the latter said, and yet the Church was free to compose additional prayers, then why, as a book of praise, may it not be supplemented by songs of praise composed by the Church?

Gibson, Begg and Martin replied: (1) There is such a thing as divinely instituted public worship under the New Testament as in the Old Testament dispensation. (2) Within that divinely instituted public worship there is a peculiar ordinance of song. (3) There is a divinely provided Book of Song, which was never revoked, nor ever provided with a supplement.

These men had of course to answer the claim that Paul's instruction to the Ephesian and Colossian Churches to praise God in terms of 'psalms and hymns and spiritual songs' permits the inclusion of uninspired hymns in Christian worship. The reply was, in substance, two-fold: (1) These three names 'psalms, hymns, spiritual songs', or the Hebrew and Greek terms they are derived from, occur frequently in the Book of Psalms to describe one or another of the Psalms themselves. (2) If anyone objects to the claim that these names as quoted by Paul refer in point of fact to the Book of Psalms, how will he prove that they do not?

This second point may sound like the clever answer which makes no serious contribution to a debate. Actually it should be seen as going to the heart of the issue. Given the regulative principle of worship, that nothing is to be included in the worship of God except what is prescribed in Scripture, then it is plainly not sufficient to speculate that Paul's phrase 'psalms, hymns and spiritual songs' may perhaps, or may very well, allow for uninspired hymns. The matter has to be demonstrated beyond reasonable doubt. The deciding factor in all cases where the Church's syllabus of worship is in question must be proven Biblical authority.

WORSHIP AND AUTHORITY

What distinguished the work of the Reformers as much as anything was their ceaseless concern to obtain divine authority for everything they did and taught. Hard on their heels in that respect were the Westminster Divines whose personal contendings led them to highlight the need for a divine mandate in all matters of worship. Thus they prefaced their Directory for Public Worship with the statement, 'Our care hath been to hold forth such things as are of divine institution'. For them that meant Biblical authority. The unadorned but supremely clear and effective language of their Catechism, indicating the place given to the Bible in this connection, is well known: 'The Word of God which is contained in the Scriptures of the Old and New Testaments is the only rule to direct us how we may glorify and enjoy Him.'

The temptation is always there to short-circuit this foundation principle of worship and to seek pragmatic solutions to questions concerning worship which are strictly theological; or to shelter unthinkingly behind the views held about worship (on one side or another) by some good man of former days. It is a better option to wrestle with the basic principles involved – every question being brought to the bar of Holy Scripture – and to apply the conclusions faithfully.

4

Praise: The Melody of Religion

A.P.W. FRASER

The Disruption of 1843 brought no dramatic changes into the worship of the Church. What was true of its doctrine of public worship was true also of the praise offered by its people through the medium of metrical psalmody.

In order to participate in that worship they required no new words – as the people had done, for example, at the time of the Reformation. They already had in their own language the familiar words of the Psalms, in the Scottish Metrical Version of 1650. New tunes were not an immediate necessity either – as they had been at the time of the Reformation. But, in the case of the tunes, the story is not quite so straightforward.

It is a fascinating and significant story; and to tell it is the business of this chapter. In order to learn its lessons we have to go some way further back in history than 1843.

HISTORICAL ORIGINS

For a Church which recognises the worship of the Jewish synagogue as a major influence on the development of its own mode of worship the fact that the best musical authorities of our day are united in tracing the history of all Christian Church music back to the synagogue cannot be without interest.

To give an exact description of the music of the New Testament Church is, of course, impossible. The Church's melodies were not written down in any way until the sixth century, and musical notation with any similarity to what we know today was not invented until the eleventh century. It would be reasonable to assume, however, that, in singing God's praise, the early Christians would be inclined to use the melodies that were already familiar to many of them – the cantillations of the synagogue. Although it has not always been recognised to have been the case, recent musicological research strongly supports the conclusion that that is exactly what they did.

The singing in the synagogue differed from the singing in the Temple in two important ways: it was unaccompanied, and the congregation were fully involved. All the indications are that the early Church sang in the same way. It is also worth noting that, surrounded as it was by Greek culture with its famous music, the Church stood apart. It not only chose the music of the synagogue rather than the music of the Greek temple; it opted for music which grew out of a context of worship rather than the entertainment music of which there was an abundance at the time.

Debate soon arose about the desirability of using instruments in worship. The arguments in favour were rejected, 'With the result that the music composed for the Church during the first thousand years or so was sung unaccompanied' (Harman and Mellers, *Man and his Music*, 1962, p.2). Hymns also became popular in some places at an early date, but, 'In the second half of the third century there was a general suppression of non-biblical hymns, caused by the dangerous popularity of heretical compositions. Psalm-singing was promoted instead' (David Hiley in *New Oxford Companion to Music*, 1983, vol 2. p.1447).

In spite of these factors the simplicity of the early Church's worship was soon lost. David Hiley, again, explains: 'Chants for congregational singing – for example psalm tones and hymns – have retained a simple and direct character. But practically all other chants have come down to us in a form for trained choirs or solo singers, relatively ornate in style and rather remote or "other worldly" in character'. The story of how plain chant developed is, of course, musically fascinating. It is the embryo out of which the whole of Western music grew. But its suitability for worship is another matter. Erik Routley sums up the lesson of a thousand years in three sentences: 'Once the Church became an established public institution, congregational singing was unknown in it, and it remained unknown until a very late stage in the Middle Ages. The music appropriate to the Mass and to the monastic offices was sung always by a cantor with a choir and only overheard by the lay worshipper. If then plain song music "sounds uncongregational" to the modern ear, that is what it was meant to be' (*The Music of Christian Hymns*).

The Reformation immediately produced a new kind of music which is a study in itself. For the purposes of this chapter, the first point to notice is the obvious one that the Reformation gave the music of the Church back to the people. It was to become the part of public worship in which they especially participated.

The hymns of Martin Luther are widely acknowledged to have been influential in spreading the doctrines of the Reformation. The tunes (chorales) to which they were sung were of a generally high standard (Luther himself was an able musician). Their musical character was strongly influenced by plainsong – Luther 'regarded medieval music not as something to be swept away, but as something to be used with restraint and discrimination' (Routley, *op. cit.*). The secular songs of the Minnesinger were also an obvious influence. These were tunes for the congregation to sing, although their idiom owed more to the music of the aristocracy than of the ordinary people.

The Swiss Reformation produced music of a different character. Those who wish to study the subject further will find a great deal of interesting material in the general histories and dictionaries of music as well as the writings of specialists in this field; but the work of Erik Routley is outstandingly useful (especially *The Music of Christian Hymnody*, 1957, and *The Music of Christian Hymns*, 1981). The main point to grasp is that the difference in the music was a reflection of the difference in theological emphasis between Luther and Calvin and their respective colleagues.

In Switzerland the words the people were given to sing in their own language were the words of the psalms – in metrical versions. The first of these were written by the distinguished poet Clement Marot, and they became very popular in the French Court. Modified versions of some of them came into John Calvin's hands during his brief exile in Strasbourg, and he was sufficiently impressed to include twelve of them along with five versions of his own in the Psalter he published there in 1539. Strasbourg was, in fact, the birthplace of the great Reformed tradition of metrical psalmody.

Along with these vernacular psalm versions, a new kind of music began to emerge. Referring to one of the most famous Strasbourg tunes, PSALM 36, Routley says, here 'you have something totally unlike the Lutheran chorale'. Having demonstrated this in a penetrating musical analysis, he concludes: 'If we want to put all this untechnically we should say that this is a wholly "congregational" tune: it may be one of the longest hymn tunes ever written, but it at once captures a universal quality of singableness which the Lutheran tunes very rarely have. Few Lutheran tunes were ever "exported" until very much later. This one began to travel at once' (*Music of Christian Hymns*).

In 1541 Calvin was able to return to Geneva and immediately applied himself to the task of establishing metrical psalmody as the practice of the Church there. The most important psalters were published in 1551 (83 metrical psalms – 49 by Marot, 34 by Theodore Beza) and in 1562 (all 150 psalms – 49 by Marot, the rest all by Beza – in no less than 110 different metres).

Musically the 1551 Psalter is of the very greatest importance. Its musical editor was Louis Bourgeois, who was cantor of St. Peter's Church in Geneva from 1545 to 1553. Of its 85 tunes he tells us he composed 34 himself and adapted another 36. Numerous compliments have been paid to him. Routley's estimate is typically to-the-point: 'He was a Protestant convert who had great facility in the art of the song-writer. He does not stand high in the company of the great polyphonists of the sixteenth century; but his art was just what Calvin was looking for' (*Music of Christian Hymnody*). He had left Geneva, and probably died, before the complete psalter was published in 1562. The 40 new tunes in that psalter may have been by his successor at St. Peter's, Pierre Dubuisson, but this is not certain.

The influence of this music on the subsequent history of congregational song has been far-reaching. Bourgeois has even been described as 'the father of the modern hymn tune'. What kind of music was it? Why did it become so popular and arouse so much enthusiasm?

Clearly it was less sophisticated than the music of the Lutheran chorale. Yet it did not achieve its popularity by adopting the secular tunes of the day. This has sometimes been alleged, and Marot's psalms certainly were sung to such tunes. But, so far as the psalters were concerned, the position has been authoritatively clarified by French musicologist Pierre Pidoux in his great two-volume work *Le Psautier Huguenot* (1962). *The New Grove Dictionary* (1980) sums up his findings with the conclusion: 'It is known that Louis Bourgeois and the other creators of the Calvinist melodies did not use the French chanson repertory as a principal source of melodies for the psalter'. Plainsong – as Bourgeois himself acknowledged – was, in fact, a stronger influence, although not to anything like the same extent as it was in the music of the Lutherans.

Evidently the psalter composers had created a music which was essentially simple and approachable, and at the same time of excellent quality. It was lively, and at the same time dignified. It was modest, and at the same time had an expressive range suited to the varied sentiments of the psalms. It was contemporary, and at the same time had its roots in church tradition. It was music which clearly caught the spirit of the Genevan Reformation itself.

Obviously the melodies in these psalters were not in the same form as the melodies of the early Church. That could never have met the needs of a sixteenth century congregation. But all the available evidence points to the conclusion that the musical ideals embodied in the Reformation melodies were remarkably similar to those of the New Testament Church.

The means by which the influence of Genevan psalmody reached Scotland was, of course, the return of those who had fled to the Continent to escape persecution at home. Along with the refugees from England they had produced a series of English language metrical psalters from 1556 to 1561. Several writers contributed versions of the psalms. Who composed the tunes we do not know; but the influence of the French psalters is evident, although it was limited by the requirement for mainly Double Common Metre tunes.

Returning home the exiles made a large contribution to the English Psalter of 1562 and the Scottish Psalter of 1564. The Scottish Psalter interestingly had greater variety of metre than the English Psalter – as many as twenty-seven different metres. It also had greater musical scope than the English Psalter – 105 tunes, compared with 62. Many editions followed, of which two are especially noteworthy. The 1615 edition contained not only 'proper tunes' (i.e. one for each psalm); it also contained a selection of twelve 'common tunes', each of which could be pressed into service for use with a number of psalms – an innovation no doubt welcome to those whose musical ability was rather limited. Most distinguished of all was the 1635 edition – a remarkable collection of the best tunes to which the 1564 version was sung. It should be noted that although the famous 'Guide and Godlie Ballatis' of the Wedderburn brothers – including metrical psalms of Lutheran origin – had earlier been sung to secular melodies, the case of the psalters was different, as Millar Patrick records: 'The secular style . . . does not appear, nor is the folk-song element allowed to intrude' (*Four Centuries of Scottish Psalmody*, 1949). The 1635 Psalter may not have achieved Genevan standards, but it was not unworthy to stand in the same tradition, and was at least comparable in quality – if not, indeed, in some respects superior – to the excellent psalters of the English Puritans.

While, however, the Puritan psalters became the fountainhead of all British congregational song, the 1635 Scottish Psalter was soon forgotten. There were two obvious reasons: in the first place, the 1564 version of the psalms was superseded only fifteen years later; and, secondly, there was a decline, not only in church music but in all music, taking place in Scotland at the time – a decline from which there was no real recovery until late in the nineteenth century.

The new version of 1650 – although it employed fewer metres – had exceptional merits, which have won it a unique place in the affections of Scottish Presbyterians. (The remarkable story of its creation is well told in Millar Patrick, chapters 8 and 9.) The sad thing about this version is that, although it was intended to be sung, it was published without tunes.

Numerous stories have been told of the allegedly barbarous fashion in which praise was rendered in the Presbyterian churches in Scotland for a hundred years and more. It is difficult to believe that the deficiencies were so widespread or so grave as they are often made to appear. That there were real deficiencies, however, it would be impossible to deny.

CONTEMPORARY BACKGROUND

Although real recovery in the music of the nation did not even commence until the closing years of the nineteenth century, a new interest in singing and especially singing in church can be traced back to the year 1753. Such splendid singing was to be heard amongst the soldiers of the 20th Foot Regiment stationed in Aberdeen, that arrangements were made for the release of their gifted teacher, Thomas Channon, from army service, in order to allow the wider community to benefit from his talents. He gave his time to training large numbers of people to sing and formed church choirs, first at Monymusk, and then in a number of different centres in the North East. John Wesley, on a visit to the area, was greatly impressed with the quality of the singing, and the enthusiasm aroused was such that the Town Councils of Glasgow and Edinburgh heard of it and appointed teachers to promote similar standards of singing there.

It is a relief to know that, in some places at least, real improvements in congregational singing began to follow; but Reformed piety cannot take satisfaction from all that was happening in Scottish church music in the early years of the nineteeth century. This has been called 'The Era of the Great Precentors'. The very name, with its implications of over-emphasis on musical performance, creates a sense of unease. Should this be a primary concern of those who gather for worship?

With that qualification, it has to be recorded that there were a number of leading figures who, to a greater or lesser degree, had a beneficial influence on the psalmody of the Scottish church. The first of these is R.A. Smith. He was precentor of Paisley Abbey from 1807 to 1823 – its musical reputation continues to this day – and from 1823 to 1829 he was precentor of St. George's Church in Edinburgh. In collaboration with a musical minister, Dr. Andrew Thomson, he raised the singing to high standards. While Dr. Thomson himself is remembered as the composer of the tune ST. GEORGE'S, EDINBURGH, Smith's was undoubtedly the more significant musical talent. Henry Farmer rates him, 'The most outstanding composer of his day in the Presbyterian Church' (*History of Music in Scotland*, 1947) and the tunes SELMA, ST. LAWRENCE and MORVEN are certainly reason for gratitude, even if INVOCATION is less so.

Three other Edinburgh precentors became especially famous: John Templeton of Broughton Place Secession Church, where the esteemed preacher and expositor Dr. John Brown was minister, John Wilson of St. Mary's Church of Scotland, and David Kennedy of Nicolson Street United Presbyterian Church. Commemorative bronze plaques on the steps from Waterloo Place leading to the Calton Hill indicate how highly respected it was possible for precentors to be at the time. The Glasgow precentors whose names are most familiar to us today are probably Neil Dougal, composer of KILMARNOCK, Robert Simpson, composer or adapter of BALLERMA, and Hugh Wilson, composer of MARTYRDOM. Other centres also had their notable precentors. One of those from Aberdeen, Donald Reid, evidently led the singing at the Free Church Assembly in Inverness in 1845.

Other Scottish musicians of the time who should not escape our attention include John Turnbull, composer of TORWOOD, William Broomfield, composer of ST. KILDA, and Charles Hutcheson, composer of ARGYLE and STRACATHRO. The German musician Joseph Mainzer did a great deal in a short time to raise singing standards;

in the preface to his *Standard Psalmody of Scotland* (1845) he reproved the Scots for their neglect of their Reformation psalm tunes; and he left us the admirable tune MAINZER. More influential than any of these was North-East musician William Carnie, a vigorous campaigner for better musical standards who taught large classes to sing. He published a series of what he called 'Fly-leaves of Hymn and Psalm Tunes', which grew into the Northern Psalter of 1872 and included the tune CRIMOND.

LEADING FIGURES

It is time to speak of the Disruption Church itself, and the leading figure here is without question Thomas Legerwood Hately. It would be difficult to speak too highly of this admirable man and what he did for psalmody, in the Free Church and beyond. It is gratifying that Millar Patrick recognises the significance of what he attempted: 'His aim was an advance on R.A. Smith's: it was not at choir singing, but at singing by the congregation' (*ibid.*).

Born in Greenlaw in 1815, he moved early in life to Edinburgh where he found employment in the printing industry. His family background favoured the early development of a love for music, and he soon acquired good singing experience and a useful general knowledge of music. At the age of twenty-one he was appointed precentor of North Leith Parish Church. He married happily, and it was his wife who dissuaded him from pursuing the career of a professional singer. When she died, after only eight years of marriage, he emerged from the experience of that painful providence resolved to give up his employment in printing and devote all his energy to the promotion of psalmody.

He was already, by this time, a Free Churchman. His evangelical convictions led him to identify with the Disruption Church, and he was immediately appointed Precentor to the General Assembly – a position he held until his death in 1867. The Free Church also had other work for him to do. Its first psalter, *The Psalmody of the Free Church of Scotland* was published in 1845. Hately edited this in collaboration with the distinguished music critic and historian George Hogarth. Even allowing for the fact that they were following on work which had already been done within the Church of Scotland, it is remarkable that they had a psalter of such quality in print so soon after the Disruption.

1845 must have been a very busy year. It also saw the publication of 'The National Psalmist' which was identical with the above except that it included 'A short and easy guide to psalm-singing by T.L. Hately'. In the same year the General Assembly commissioned him to record in writing the Gaelic Long Tunes and this was soon published as *Old Gaelic Psalm Tunes taken down by T.L. Hately*.

It is more understandable how he could maintain this kind of work-rate after 1847 when he gave himself full-time to the work of psalmody, and it becomes impossible within the scope of a chapter like this, to describe all his publications. The most important by far was the new psalter issued by authority of the General Assembly: *The Scottish Psalmody* of 1854. Hately was in effect the musical editor.

Such editorial work was only one part of Hately's contribution to the improvement of the Church's psalmody. The provision of a suitable psalter will not achieve much unless congregations are introduced to its contents, and also, preferably, taught something about singing. That there was still a need for such teaching is indicated by a quotation Millar Patrick gives from 'The Scottish Guardian' of May 1848: 'The instances of ignorance and bad taste to which the ear is bound to listen in church singing are innumerable. Some shout at the utmost pitch of their voice, some wheeze with their breath, some sing through their nose, others with clenched teeth'. Hugh Miller expressed similar views even more forcibly in *The Witness*.

Hately commenced congregational psalmody classes in 1846. Gatherings for psalm-singing led by Hately were convened during the General Assembly. These 'Aggregate Meetings', as they were called, aroused great interest. The 1850 Assembly resolved, on the recommendation of the Psalmody Committee, 'That Mr. Hately be sent forth on a mission of musical instruction, over the country, among the churches'. He travelled widely, regularly gathering classes of 500 or 600, and, in the case of Greenock, 900.

These were not mere singing classes. By the standards of his day Hately had quite a wide knowledge of music, an acquaintance with the history of church music, and a special enthusiasm for the music of the Reformation. He made a point of passing on something of this knowledge in all his classes, and made especially thorough preparation of material to be presented to the Aggregate Meetings during the Assembly. He was frequently invited to give lectures on different aspects of psalmody – and not only in various churches around the land: in May 1851 he drew a large audience to a public lecture in the Hopetoun Rooms in Queen Street, Edinburgh, on 'The History of Psalmody'.

His son, Walter Hately, was able to say of his father's work, 'What impresses one most of all is the unerring instinct with which he brought forward all that is best in church music and psalmody, and revolutionised the taste of his day' (*A Scottish Psalmodist*, 1908). This short biography is concluded with a long tribute from Alex T. Niven, who was Convener of the Church of Scotland Committee on Psalmody. It refers to 'his powers of teaching' as 'something wonderful', and mentions the high commendation his work received from HM Inspector of Schools. It speaks of his varied musical interests and continues:

'But after all it was in his work for Psalmody improvement that your father most conspicuously shone. When one remembers the trash, under the name of Psalm tunes, which used to be sung thirty years ago, and compares those with the tunes now in use in our churches, the contrast is most surprising'.

He pays tribute to Hately's knowledge of the history of psalmody, his editorial work, his compositions, and concludes: 'Altogether your father did more for the improvement of Psalmody in Scotland than any man of his time'.

No one today would claim that Hately was an outstanding composer, but it is fitting that we continue to sing his tunes, GLENCAIRN, LEUCHARS and CUNNINGHAM (the last composed in memory of William Cunningham at the suggestion of 'Rabbi' Duncan).

The other leading figure of the Disruption Church whose contribution to psalmody is of outstanding importance is Rev. Neil Livingston (1803–1891), minister at Stair in Ayrshire from 1844 to 1886. He gave service as Clerk, and later Convener, of the Psalmody Committee and was particularly active in promoting psalmody as part of the Church's educational programme. His outstanding achievement, however, was the publication in 1864 of a scholarly edition of the great Scottish Psalter of 1635. While Hately's contribution was mainly to the psalmody of his own time, Livingston's work endures, and is, to this day, the admiration of all students of Scottish church music. The Preface and Dissertations in this volume are essential reading for anyone intending to take the history of psalmody seriously. Sadly the present day Free Church does not possess a copy – a deficiency which, it must be hoped, will one day be made good.

A Free Church musician who is less well known, A.D. Thomson, who taught music at the Normal College for the training of teachers in Glasgow, should probably be mentioned, if only because he appears to have been the composer of the now popular tune FREE CHURCH.

THE PSALTERS

The fact that the Free Church had already achieved the publication of a psalter by 1845 is surely some indication of the importance it attached to psalmody. Amongst the many pressing matters calling for its attention it included the improvement of the praise in its congregations.

This publication, *The Psalmody of the Free Church of Scotland*, was, like many in its day, purely a tune-book. The words of the psalms were not included. The tunes were in four-part harmony, printed in staff notation in open score. (Although various sight-reading aids were by then beginning to appear, John Curwen did not publish his system of sol-fa notation until 1863.)

The Address and Preface are informative. The Address speaks of the desirability of an authorised psalter as a unifying influence in the Church's psalmody. It states that a characteristic of this book is that, 'It discards all theatrical and jig-like, and almost all repeating tunes, which, if admissible in secular meetings, are justly deemed out of place in the house of God'. The Preface briefly outlines the historic sources of metrical psalmody and then laments: 'But in most modern collections the ore is buried and lost among the dross. A spurious kind of psalmody has been introduced, which threatens to destroy the character and prevent the object of church music'. It cites, for example, 'Psalm tunes made out of popular ballads, and even out of airs taken from the most profane productions of the stage'.

By contrast, the editors announce, 'It has been our object that the contents of this little book shall consist chiefly of the old and venerable tunes established in this country since the day of the Reformation, with the addition only of such among more modern tunes, as are in the true style and spirit of psalmody, and have been sanctioned by general use'.

An analysis of the contents – a total of 83 tunes – reveals that, although there are not so many tunes from the post-Reformation psalters as might be expected, the editors have largely succeeded in realising their aims. It is interesting that this psalter contains commendations from two distinguished London musicians – Edward Taylor, Gresham Professor of Music, and James Turle of Westminster Abbey.

The next Free Church psalter was *The Scottish Psalmody* of 1854. It was in the same format as its predecessor – still basically a tune-book, although, curiously, the first verse of a psalm portion is interlined with each tune. The repertoire was now greatly extended – 123 tunes in the first edition, increasing, as supplements were added in later editions, to 151 tunes and then 183 tunes. Intriguingly, not only did each supplement have its own separate alphabetical order, the 123 tunes of the first edition are divided – numbers 1–67 in alphabetical order, and 68–123 with a separate alphabetical order. The explanation is: Tunes 1–67 'have been chosen from lists sent in by ministers and laymen in various parts of the country'. As for tunes 68–123, 'After providing all the tunes called for by the country, a considerable number of tunes, both from home and from foreign sources, hitherto little known, have been introduced, to which particular attention is called'.

This information not only reveals the aims – and the tact – of the editors; it may help to preserve the sanity of anyone who has the courage to explore the bewildering profusion of psalters published around this time. Most of them were based on *The Scottish Psalmody*, and most of them were unauthorised by any church. It was an age when publishers found that issuing metrical psalters was an attractive commercial proposition.

So what of the tunes in this influential psalter? There are a few more tunes from Reformation days – although the editors still missed several which have since become well known. The inclusion of a considerable number from German sources seems to indicate a failure to grasp the real difference between Lutheran and Reformed music. There is a very commendable increase in the number of strong tunes from the eighteenth century – of necessity most of them from England, but the four Scottish tunes from that century which have since gained recognition, BALFOUR, GLASGOW, MONTROSE and ST. PAUL, are all here. Not many of the additional nineteenth century tunes have survived, but it is good to see EVAN and KILMARNOCK making an appearance, and the number of tunes by Hately himself is increased. Altogether less happy is the apparent reversal of earlier policy involved in the increased number of repeating tunes.

For its day, this psalter must be judged a considerable achievement. It was generally recognised as the best of its generation, and its influence went far beyond the Free Church. Rev. J.W. Mackmeeken of Lesmahagow went so far in his *History of the Scottish Metrical Psalms* (1872), as to say it created 'quite an era in the history of modern music'. (Quoted by Henry Farmer.)

Another publication which appeared in the same year should perhaps receive a passing mention. It was *The Book of Psalms and Sacred Harmonies* edited by T.L. Hately. Of this his son said with some excitement, 'While outwardly the book has the appearance of only one volume, it contains two separate volumes under one binding – above, the Psalms in metre, and, below, the admirable collection of tunes known as *The Scottish Psalmody*. Any part of the one may be opened simultaneously with the other, forming one page'. So appeared the first of many split-page psalters. The idea was Hately's.

A considerably altered *Scottish Psalmody* was adopted by the Free Church in 1873, and was in turn replaced by 'The Scottish Psalter' in 1883. Since neither of these have significantly influenced the Free Church in the twentieth century it is not necessary to attempt an analysis of their contents.

GAELIC PSALMODY

Before proceeding further it is necessary to turn our attention to a type of psalm-singing which is largely independent of the tune-books or musical notation of any kind. This is the oral tradition of Gaelic psalmody. A writer who does not speak Gaelic is even more dependent on the knowledge and advice of others in this area than in other aspects of the subject, but no account of Free Church psalmody could afford to overlook the distinctive and remarkable singing of its Gaelic-speaking people.

Gaelic psalmody, of course, was no more created by the Disruption than any other kind of psalmody, nor is it restricted to the Free Church, although it is mainly found there. Its origins are to be traced to the meeting of the Synod of Argyll at Rothesay in May 1653. The Synod, being concerned to provide for the Gaelic-speaking people of the Highlands, desired 'that the psalms be turned to Irish mitre, so as they may be soonge with the comon toones', and ordained that there should be a Gaelic translation. The first fifty of these metrical psalms (the Caogad) were issued six years later, and the whole psalter in 1694.

The fact that these metrical psalms were all in common metre, to fit 'the Lowland tunes', sometimes appears to be emphasised in order to make the point that the resulting psalmody was an imposition from outside Gaeldom, a musical hybrid, or even a mere 'marginal survival' of something which is not at all distinctively Gaelic. Such views seem to underestimate a fundamental factor: the nature of folk culture and the manner in which it develops. Gaelic psalmody is by no means the first, nor the last, folk-music to absorb elements from another culture and make them wholly its own.

This process can be observed in each of the main aspects of this music. 'Putting-out-the-line' by the precentor is not uniquely Gaelic, nor did it originate in the Highlands. It is practised by West Indian pentecostals in what they call 'tracked hymns'. Black Baptist churches in the United States have a practice which they call 'Dr. Watts' or 'Long Metre' (cf. the Scottish term 'Long Tunes'), and the old Regular Baptist Churches in eastern Kentucky apparently come closer than that in resemblance to the singing of the Gaelic precentors (see T.E. Miller, article on Oral Psalmody in *Journal of the Hymn Society of America*, January 1984). To say, however, that putting-out-the-line is not unique to Gaeldom, even in our own day, is not at all to say that the practice which the Highland precentors have developed within their own tradition is anything else but distinctively Gaelic.

So far as the historical origin of lining out is concerned, there is no evidence of its existence prior to the Westminster Assembly (see Nicholas Temperly in *Journal of the Hymn Society of America*, July 1984, and also articles on Metrical Psalmody in *The New Grove Dictionary* (1980). The Scottish commissioners were opposed to it, but acquiesced in a recommendation in 'The Directory for Public Worship' that, 'for the present, where many in the Congregation cannot read, it is convenient'. This temporary expedient became quite widespread in England, Scotland and America, and when the psalms appeared in Gaelic translation, the same practice, for obvious reasons, was followed. The fact that a temporary expedient has become a permanent feature of Gaelic psalm-singing may have two explanations. Morag Macleod, of the School of Scottish Studies in Edinburgh, offers one: 'The recommendation of the 1746 General Assembly that there should be a "return to the ancient practice of singing without reading the line" was difficult to implement in the Highlands, where the less "ancient" custom had become part of the Reformed tradition and where congregations were not attracted to the use of unrelieved quatrains of the still unfamiliar ballad metre'.

(Notes accompanying LP record 'Gaelic Psalm Tunes from Lewis'; Tangent Records, 1975.) Another explanation may be the extent to which the precentors were developing a style which was particularly meaningful to the congregations. Their known ability to indicate through their chant the mood and sentiments of the psalm that is being sung surely evinces a blend of musicianship and spirituality which is an example for precentors to emulate wherever they serve.

Turning to the part the congregation play in this mode of praise, the folk-music process may be observed in two ways. In the first place, because the melodies for which the Gaelic metrical versions were intended came from outside Gaelic culture, their tonality, in some cases especially, felt unfamiliar to the Gaelic ear. As a consequence, in process of time they were spontaneously modified to bring them more into line with Gaelic melodic tradition.

Secondly, in addition to modifying the basic melodies, Gaelic singers instinctively began to ornament them. In itself, of course, melodic ornamentation, in both vocal and instrumental music, is widespread in many cultures, and the particular type of ornamentation in which the Gaelic ear delights is not unique either. This involves each individual in the congregation adding, in his or her own way, to the expressiveness of the tune through both melodic elaboration and rhythmic freedom. The remarkable sonorities which result arc similar to what musicians call discordant heterophony. (Strictly speaking, heterophony is the singing or playing of a melody simultaneously with its variation.) Musicologists have not so far established how significant historical precedents may be. What is clear is that this music developed through a process that can still be observed. The increasing elaboration to which all ornamentation tends resulted in the six 'Long Tunes' written down and published by Joseph Mainzer in 1844, and later, with more understanding by T.L. Hately (1845) and F.W. Whitehead (1909).

These were still sung in parts of Caithness, Sutherland, Ross-shire and Inverness-shire in the earlier part of this century, but their use in church has now entirely died out. The process that created them, however, still goes on in the western mainland, and in the Hebrides especially, where it is noticeable that tunes which have been in use for a long time have become more elaborate than tunes more recently brought into the repertoire. Heterophonic singing is to be found in other church traditions – Ambrosian chant may be one of the most interesting examples (see Elliot and Rimmer, *History of Music in Scotland*, 1973, p.8) – but there is no doubt the Gael has a particular genius for this kind of music, which may well be related to the elaboration in other Celtic art-forms.

Such a description of Gaelic psalmody may seem to raise the question, How does all this fit in with the Reformed tradition of metrical psalm-singing described in the rest of the chapter? The musical form may seem to be dissimilar – more like the responsorial psalmody of the Medieval Church than the metrical psalmody of the Reformers. The elaboration of the melody, especially, may seem to be in contrast with the elemental simplicity of the strongly congregational tunes of the Reformation. The overall character of this music may seem more subjective than the more disciplined and poised music of the Reformed psalters.

The answer must surely be, in the first place, that it is only to be expected that the working out of Reformed principles in different cultures will produce some differences of detail in practice. Thus, if the churches of the Reformation knew nothing like the chant of the Gaelic precentors, the Synagogue certainly did. Responsorial psalmody may not have been the musical form chosen by the Reformers, but it was familiar to the Synagogue congregation.

The melodies of Gaelic psalmody also may not be so far removed in character from the melodies of Reformation psalmody as at first they seem. Obviously, although some people may want to say a more culturally enlightened Synod of Argyll would have chosen different metres for the Gaelic psalms so that they could be sung to indigenous melodies, the result of what they did is that – like the early Christians, and like the Reformers – Gaelic worshippers have music which came out of a context of worship rather than secular folk-song; and a musical link has been established between them and the international family of Reformed Churches, which may not be so inappropriate after all.

Having adapted these melodies to make them more meaningful in their own culture, they have used them, it may be suggested, in a way which is essentially Reformed. They make abundant use of melodic elaboration; but the effect, as has been shown, is not really complexity, it is simple melody against a background of kaleidoscopic sound. Although the music fostered by the Reformers was the music of strong, simple melody, in spite of the misgivings of John Calvin and some others, they never insisted on bare melody without harmony. In Reformed tradition harmony has always tended to be around. It was positively promoted by the Disruption leaders. And if harmony is appropriate, why not the discordant heterophony of the Gael just as much as the diatonic harmony of other cultures?

There is another way in which an instinctive insistence on simplicity may be detectable in Gaelic practice. Why, it may be asked, did the famous six 'Long Tunes' fall out of use? Was it because the acceptable limits of melodic ornamentation had been reached – or perhaps exceeded? It is well known that in some places today a highly ornamented type of psalmody is practised in the home. It is of very real musicological interest, but it has not found favour in public worship.

Finally the spirit which is expressed in this psalmody is readily identifiable as the spirit of Reformed piety. This is apparent not only to those who belong to the culture, but also to those from outside it. The distinguished Scottish musicologist Francis Collinson has described this music in his standard work *The Traditional and National Music of Scotland* (1966); but he has especially placed us in his debt with an article – one of a series – in *The Scotsman* of 26 November 1960. It includes the following:

'The attitude and demeanour of the precentor in these Highland churches is impressive. Often he sings with eyes closed, rolling out the softly sonorous Gaelic of the Psalm from memory, sometimes in a curious nasal quality of voice reminiscent of the old Puritans. The Congregation sing in unison as is the custom of the Gael, but with the melody profusely ornamented with grace notes ('slurs' they call them), each singer improvising his or her own pattern of ornamentation of the tune as the spirit moves him.

'The result is astonishing, for it creates a shimmering kaleidoscopic harmony of its own, a harmony which bears a strange resemblance to the echoing acoustics of a cathedral, and against which the tune stands out in great strength and dignity. In the slow quantitative rather than rhythmic measure of the tune, it is almost unavoidable that some voices should move on to the next note before others, and the resulting effect is obviously one which the Congregation like to create deliberately for the sake of its further clashing harmonies.

'To crown the whole musical structure, the precentor often breaks in with the next line before the Congregation have come to the end of theirs, causing a further deliberate collision of tones. From the description, one might imagine that it must result in ear-splitting cacophony; in actual fact the whole effect is of quite astonishing and unforgettable beauty.'

CONTINUING RELEVANCE

No attempt has been made in this chapter to give a full description of psalmody in the nineteenth century Free Church. Attention has been focused rather on the outlook and practice of the Church as it emerged from the Disruption itself. That serves to highlight a number of issues of the very greatest relevance to the Free Church a hundred and fifty years later, and indeed to all who practise metrical psalmody whatever their situation.

First and foremost, the leaders responsible for giving direction to the psalmody of the Disruption Church were conscious of their theological identity and heritage. They could not have been further from regarding the type and quality of music employed in the worship of the Church as a matter of indifference. It should be music which stood in the historic tradition of metrical psalmody. For that reason they gave a prominent place to the tunes of the Reformation psalters and their successors, and endeavoured to ensure that the more recent tunes they included were of similar character. This in no way meant that their music was out-of-date. There was a large proportion of contemporary tunes in their psalters, including some they composed themselves.

Musical quality was an important consideration to them. They strove to attain this by two methods. The first was publishing psalters in which they set themselves high standards. Clearly they considered these psalters essential to the task of encouraging the use of tunes which were of better quality than many currently in circulation. Secondly, they embarked on a vigorous programme of education. The publication of psalters will not accomplish much if those for whom they are intended do not know how to use them. The Disruption Church, therefore, aimed to give much-needed guidance to precentors, and to teach congregations not only to sing better, but to appreciate what is best in metrical psalmody. Children were given instruction, not only in church but also in school and, to make this more effective, psalmody instruction in colleges of education was given high priority.

In all this it is very obvious that, although they understood popular taste and related well to ordinary people, they did not consider popular fashion should dictate the character of the Church's psalmody any more than it should determine its mode of worship, or any other aspect of its doctrine or practice. Their Reformed instincts led them to see the teaching of psalmody as a part – and not an unimportant part – of the overall teaching responsibility of the Church. It was a responsibility they were not inclined to abdicate.

The twentieth century Free Church with its greatly reduced resources was not well placed to carry forward the work of post-Disruption days. A brave attempt was made with the publication of a psalter in 1910, retaining the title, *The Scottish Psalmody*. In its Preface it claims to draw on the 1635 Scottish Psalter, and incorporates an unacknowledged quotation from Neil Livingston. Its selection from that source, however, differs only slightly from what is in the Disruption psalters, without being any larger. Commendably it observes, 'It is hoped that the tunes from this source will be again revived'. Less commendably it endeavoured to revive repeating tunes which had fallen out of use. Of fourteen tunes by the Convener of the Psalmody Committee and one of his friends only one, ERICSTANE, has survived. The total number of tunes was 190.

The editors of the 1927 *Scottish Psalmody* indulged in drastic pruning. They added 10 tunes, but made way for them by deleting 60. Later editions added various supplements, bringing the mid-century repertoire up to 170 tunes. Along with a good deal of redundant material, many excellent tunes were lost. A considerable number of the tunes now incorporated showed little affinity with the tradition of metrical psalmody. The overall effect of this was to create a strange and regrettable anomaly. A hundred years after the Disruption, the Free Church of Scotland – the largest exclusively psalm-singing church in the land – was singing a repertoire of tunes distinguishable from the music of other churches not by its emphasis on the music of the Reformation psalters and their successors, but by something quite different. While other British churches showed a growing interest in the tunes of the historic metrical psalters, the Free Church cultivated instead the use of its own unique collection of nineteenth century American hymn tunes.

In the second half of the twentieth century it became quite an easy matter to improve on this state of affairs. Music as a whole, and church music in particular, had made such advances in the land it was a very straightforward task, even for a small church, to produce in 1977 a psalter which reflected once more the aims which the editors of the Disruption psalters had set themselves. It remains to say that the production of a psalter is no more sufficient in itself in the twentieth century than it would have been in the nineteenth. There could be no more fitting tribute to the leaders of Disruption psalmody than for the Free Church to address itself, a hundred and fifty years later, to the improvement of congregational singing with something like the vigour and discernment which they displayed.

The spirit which informed all their work is one to emulate. The rather ponderous language of the day cannot conceal it, as it is expressed in the final paragraph of the Address in their first psalter:

'In this Address, the Committee has directed its principal attention to the material or natural elements of Church singing; and for the obvious reason, that the right direction of these is its leading business. But they themselves reverently bear in mind – and it must never be forgotten – that the singing of Psalms, however perfectly executed, like the making of prayers, however eloquently expressed, is utterly worthless without grace in the heart. This great matter, however, is the work and business of the Church itself; and it shall here only be added, that the blessing of the Great Head of the church is fervently invoked, as upon all the efforts of the Free Church, so upon this humble attempt to promote His glory, by improving the singing of His praise'.

5

Beyond the Borders of Scotland: The Church's Missionary Enterprise

W.D. GRAHAM

'The Principles guiding the Free Church's Missionary endeavours in the Disruption era and the outworking of these Principles in the Free Church of Scotland today'

INTRODUCTION

John Bunyan's character 'Mr. Facing-Both-Ways', could well describe the Church in Europe in the 18th century. This 'enigmatic century' (Dr. Skevington Wood) was filled with such diverse forces which seemed to be pulling the church in different directions. It was a century when Rationalism, Latitudinarianism, (and its Scottish counterpart, Moderatism) Unitarianism and destructive Biblical Criticism had their grip on the Church in England and elsewhere. There was a decline in many areas of Church life. Dr. Thomas Chalmers called the century the 'Dark Age' of the Scottish church.

Yet, on the other hand, it was a century of revivals – of the Wesleys and Whitefield, of Charles Simeon and Jonathan Edwards, of the Moravian Brethren, of Isaac Watts and John Newton. God moved in great and gracious ways throughout Europe, Scandinavia, Great Britain and North America. As the century drew to its close strong evidence could be seen of the blessings of revival in the Church of Christ through the establishment of a great host of Missionary Agencies and Bible Societies – this was the beginning of the modern missionary movement and it led into what K.S. Latourette called 'the Great Century' for the Church.

Scotland, too, had been touched by the winds of revival during the 18th century and a strengthening evangelicalism was beginning to influence the church life of the nation. Stirrings of this new life were seen in the Church of Scotland Assembly of 1796 when the cause of Foreign Mission was brought before the Assembly.

The issue was shelved at that time in spite of the famous interjection of Dr. John Erskine to reason from the Bible as to the

Christian duty to take the Gospel to those still 'sitting in darkness and under the shadow of death'. It would be another thirty years before the Church took this duty seriously. However from within the ranks of the Churches in Scotland many did offer themselves for missionary service through the several agencies established at the close of the century. The Glasgow Missionary Society and the Scottish Missionary Society (of Edinburgh) were established in 1796 and through them Scottish missionaries went out to India, Jamaica and South Africa. Several Scots also served the Lord through the London Missionary Society, a Society which was actively supported by Dr. Thomas Chalmers.

When the Church of Scotland did agree to establish its own missionary work, Rev. (later Dr.) Alexander Duff was the first minister to be sent out under its auspices. That was in 1827. Duff's work in India became famous and encouraged others to follow in his wake.

By the time of the Disruption in 1843 the Church of Scotland had some twenty missionaries on the foreign field, including those involved in Jewish evangelism in Europe.

While we are confining our study to the Free Church missions we must remember that other Scottish Churches also responded to the missionary challenge. The Original Secession Church, the Reformed Presbyterian Church and the United Presbyterian Church have all a stirring missionary story to tell, as has the Church of Scotland even after the events of 1843.

But let us look at the Free Church as it was at the Disruption.

THE FREE CHURCH OF 1843

When the dust of the Disruption settled what kind of Church emerged? The Free Church emerged with a distinctive character which moulded together a virile theological orthodoxy with a deep social conscience. There was abroad at the time an expanding awareness of the wider world. It was an era of colonial expansion and, in spite of the extreme poverty experienced by so many in the country, there was an awakening sense of responsibility to God for those still steeped in heathen darkness.

Many of the 'Disruption Fathers' were men of a great catholic spirit – none more so than Chalmers himself – and this brought the Free Church into contact with the leading spiritual movements of the day in Britain and the European continent. It so happened that the year 1843 was one of the 'peak' years for recruitment to the cause of foreign missions – the Disruption occurred at a time of real missionary interest.

The Free Church became heir to strong strands of deep spirituality which were the legacy of the revivals – a matter of great significance for the missionary work as some of the leading missionaries were products of this revival heritage, eg Duff and James Stewart of Lovedale, South Africa.

The Free Church also became the bastion of a deep theological orthodoxy which was yet always characterised by a warm evangelicalism and zeal for evangelism and which issued in Christian work of great quality, done by people of great Christian character.

From this background we can trace several distinct strands which show us the motives behind the missionary cause of the Free Church in 1843 and later years.

The Motives for Mission in the Free Church of Scotland at, and immediately following, 1843

The first great motive which gave thrust to the Free Church's missionary endeavour following the Disruption came from its theological convictions. This showed itself in various ways:

1. The Confessional Standards of the Church

There was a new awareness of the Confessional Standards of the Church. These had always laid upon the Church the charge, 'And this Gospel must be preached in all the world for a witness unto all nations, and then shall the end be' (Matthew 24:14) (Scots Confession of 1560). The Confession concluded with the prayer, 'Let all the nations come to thy true knowledge'. The same spirit was revealed in later documents of the church as, for example, the exhortation of the 1647 General Assembly to a concerted effort to propagate the Gospel 'to those who are without, especially the Jews'.

2. Biblical Authority and Biblical Preaching

Added to this there was the renewed emphasis on Biblical authority and Biblical preaching, with a strong evangelical flavour. It is worth noting that the earliest Free Church Missionary magazine was not for foreign missions alone but included the home missions work of the Church. The task of a Bible-based evangelism was seen as applying equally to those 'in darkness' in Scotland as well as abroad.

3. The Sovereignty of God

The resurgence of Biblical theology laid stress on the great doctrine of the Sovereignty of God and 'the Headship of Christ and his Kingship over the whole world' (Alexander Duff's phrase). The geographical horizons of people were being extended during the era of colonial expansion and this fitted in well with the renewed emphasis on the universality of God's authority and the awareness that for all men it is true that 'Salvation is found in no-one else, for there is no other name under heaven given to men by which we must be saved' (Acts 4.12).

Dr. Alexander Duff during one of his famous addresses to the Free Church General Assembly said this: 'Ah! friends, fathers and brethren, what then ought to be our resolution this night? Up – up; onward – onward, be our worldwide battle cry, under the banner and leadership of our Saviour-King! On His head – ah, that precious head! – already are many crowns; . . . But one crown is still wanting. It is the crown of all the earth . . .'

> 'Come then, and added to Thy many crowns,
> Receive yet one, the crown of all the earth,
> Thou alone art worthy!'

It is this belief in the Divine Sovereignty and the Kingship of Christ over all the nations which gives an authority to Christian missions that ought to be the hallmark of all that is undertaken in Christ's name. This was true of the missionary vision held by the 'Disruption Fathers'.

Perhaps the best illustration of this is in the life of Dr. Thomas Chalmers himself, who, following his conversion in 1811 almost immediately espoused the cause of Foreign Missions, supporting the Societies through which the missionary concern of Scottish Christians had to be channelled in those days.

When Chalmers was appointed Professor of Moral Philosophy at St. Andrews in 1823 he supported the struggling (and almost persecuted) Missionary Society there and breathed new life into it. Dr. Alexander Duff was one of the choice fruits of Chalmers' encouragement to that Society.

And Chalmers' theology was, of course, now in full sympathy with the Church's Confessions of earlier days – a theology grounded in God's Word, and reflecting God's great concern for the world he had made. Mission was a direct outcome of this.

4. The Puritan Hope

Closely allied to the foregoing was the view summed up in the title of Iain H. Murray's book *The Puritan Hope.*

With few (but notable) exceptions the eschatology of Scottish evangelicalism, as represented by the Disruption Church, was post-millenialism. This put a very distinct stamp upon the whole missionary movement of the Church. The missionaries viewed the future with optimism – the Christian optimism that, having been placed in the world to be lights for Christ and to work for the coming of His kingdom, they could concentrate upon those activities which would not only convert individuals but Christianise nations. Missionaries saw their task as foundational to a future ingathering of many to faith in Christ through the process of, first of all, concentrating on either strategic people or practices which would bear future success.

The optimism of this view of the future went well with the enthusiasm of the colonising period but must not be confused with it. It was a spiritual optimism which produced great perseverance and courage in servants of God who often had to labour long with little outward signs of success but who fully expected that God was going to do great things in days to come. It was this which gave vision to David Livingstone, John G. Paton, Dr. Alexander Duff of India and Dr James Stewart of Lovedale. Such men believed in a future great revival of Christianity bringing multitudes of men and nations to Christ.

By the end of the 19th century much of the evangelicalism had gone out of the Church's missionary vision and the post-millenialism that was left lent itself to the development of the 'social Gospel' while the evangelism was undertaken by a new 'breed' of missionaries with distinctly pre-millenarian views – such as Hudson Taylor and the early 'Keswick Movement' missionaries who saw their task as 'giving the simple gospel message to the greatest number possible of ignorant heathen in the shortest possible time' (G.W. Brooke – quoted in Brian Stanley, *The Bible and the Flag*, 1990).

5. The Stress on Biblical Revival

Another theological emphasis in the missionary movement of the Church was the stress upon Biblical revival. Both Alexander Duff and James Stewart came from homes which had been blessed through revivals. Both of these great men of God also looked longingly and prayerfully for the coming of revival in their own work. And these men experienced God's working in revival both in India and in South Africa. Dr. J. Edwin Orr states: 'The outstanding leader of the 1859 Revival in India was Dr. Alex. Duff' (*Light of the Nations*, p.184). Duff could speak of 'myriads instantaneously saved under the mighty outpourings of the Spirit of grace...'

This revival-enthusiasm was typical of many of the Church's missionaries. But it was a solidly based enthusiasm. It was said of John Macdonald of Calcutta (son of the 'Apostle of the North') that his theology was 'massive and substantial'. It was a theology grounded in the Reformed and Puritan tradition, deeply spiritual, profoundly optimistic and utterly dedicated to the glory of God and the Christian upliftment of 'the heathen'. It was always to this theology that Duff pointed prospective missionaries.

6. Love of Evangelism

One of the greatest distinctives of the best of Scottish evangelical theology has been its love of evangelism. This marked the missionary work of the early Free Church. It may seem odd to mention this with regard to any missionary enterprise. But much of the Free Church's missionary effort was centred in institutions, mainly schools. This was in line with the great aim of Christianising the nations, of laying a foundation which would bring multitudes to new birth in the 'prolific womb of the future' (Duff's phrase), by the grace of God. However, although much of the work was based in institutions, there was no lack of evangelistic zeal. Dr. Duff's school was established 'for the transformation of men, and for the training and equipping of educated Christian leaders. His Institution was to be a nursery of Christian workers, and so indeed it was' (Elizabeth G.K. Hewat, *Vision and Achievement 1796–1956*, 1960, p.69). It was Duff's opinion that the real evangelistic work in India should be carried out by Indians. Yet, in his Institution it was said that he was incapable of teaching any subject, even mathematics, without relating it to the Gospel for evangelistic purposes! Always alongside the Institutional work evangelism and church planting went ahead.

A similar work took place in South Africa at Lovedale, especially under Dr. James Stewart. Stewart's 'guiding idea was that Christianity is the universal educator and civiliser of heathen races, and that civilisation without Christianity never civilises'. And so, 'as a missionary place (Lovedale) seeks spiritual results as its highest and most permanent result, and as its primary aim' (James Wells, *Stewart of Lovedale*, 1919, p.257). 'The improvement of the soul' said Stewart, 'is the soul of all improvement.'

Dr. J.A. Mackay has said: 'To convey Christian culture and not communicate a Christian soul is to be Hellenists not Christians and to court a reaction in the next generation' (*The Vision of the Kingdom* p.88). The truth of these words has been abundantly borne out.

These great aims were typical of several other Christian institutions established by the Church, not only in Africa and India, but in the South Sea Islands where the Free Church worked in co-operation with the R.P. Church and the Presbyterian Churches of Australia and New Zealand. 'Dr. Alexander Duff of India . . . had a great love for the work in the New Hebrides' (J.G. Miller, *Live*, vol. 1, p.150). Part of the great work engaged in there followed Duff's own ideals in education: 'I applied my chief strength, as far as education was concerned, to make the natives good readers . . . One primary object was to teach them to read, that they might be able to read the Bible, and learn the will of God and the way of salvation for themselves' (Dr. J. Inglis, quoted in *Live*, vol. 1, p.113).

It is not without significance that the five missionaries who were Moderators of the General Assembly of the Free Church of Scotland between 1843 and 1900 were all renowned educators in India and Africa.

The early Free Church missionaries would not have agreed with the late Dr. Soltau of Korea that such education is the most expensive and least effective means of evangelism (*Missions at the Crossroads*, chap. 13). Evangelism in the institution, alongside the institution, and emanating from the institution was the common pattern. However, as far as the Free Church mission was concerned the post-millenialism of its early days began to be separated from the true evangelicalism of its early days and so the educational institutions lost their evangelistic thrust, continuing only as liberal-Christian Arts Colleges. In this way their early promise largely faded and their impact on the spiritual life of the young churches was minimised.

7. The Stress on Education

The stress on education has been a feature of the Scottish Church since Reformation times – from Knox's concept of a Kirk and School in every parish. One great reason for having the school was, as seen above, to teach the art of reading so that people could read and study the Scriptures. The Free Church in common with other missions eagerly availed themselves of the growing help given by the Bible Societies. Dr. Thomas Chalmers was an ardent supporter of the Bible Societies, which were established along with the many missionary agencies at the close of the 18th century. The translating, publishing, distributing and teaching of the Scriptures was a prominent feature of the early Free Church missionary work.

We may note one example. When Rev. John Ross came to South Africa in 1823 he brought with him a small printing press and set it up the day after his arrival, so commencing a fruitful literacy programme in order to teach people to read the Scriptures which were then in the process of being produced for the Xhosa-speaking peoples. Years later, John Ross's son and successor Rev. Dr. Bryce Ross was one of an excellent team of Xhosa experts who revised the Xhosa Bible, giving the people a version that has had an amazing impact upon their spiritual lives for several generations.

8. Acceptance of Mission as a Church Responsibility

One of the great features of the Free Church's missionary interest has been its acceptance of mission as a church responsibility. The Church itself is a missionary society. In 1843 the twenty Church of Scotland missionaries who came into the Free Church were readily accepted, as were several others who transferred from the missionary societies. In spite of the great responsibility the new church had for developing its structures at home it accepted without question its responsibility for spreading the Gospel abroad.

This direct missionary interest shown by the Church no doubt added a measure of spiritual life and vision to the home church and certainly gave (as it still does) an added confidence and security to the Church's missionaries abroad. The Free Church of the immediate post-Disruption period became somewhat of a model church in many ways, and not least in its missionary zeal. Yet for all that Foreign Missions remained a special interest of a relatively small number of the church people. Dr. Alex. Duff who became the Church's 'Missions Executive' often lamented before the General Assembly how meagre support for the missions was and there were years when no recruits to the various fields were forthcoming. Nonetheless the Church did produce ministers, teachers, doctors, nurses, artisans who graced the Church through their work in schools, orphanages, hospitals, theological colleges and churches. The scope of the Church's missionary work showed the depth of compassion felt for the peoples in unevangelised lands and the desire for their social upliftment as well as their conversion to Christ. This reflected the same spirit as was evident in Scotland in the compassionate concern Chalmers, Guthrie and others showed in the various schemes they employed to help the underprivileged.

9. Discipling the City

When the Scottish missionaries began their work in India they concentrated their initial efforts in the great cities, believing that from there the message of the Gospel would penetrate to the hinterland of these great centres of population. The situation in Africa was different – the people to be evangelised did not live in the cities. Nonetheless the strategy of 'discipling the city' is one that should never lie ignored. It was Pauline policy and no mission is really able to make an impact on a nation unless it seeks to win the cities for Christ.

Roger Greenway has written: 'It is high time that Calvinists begin to distinguish themselves more clearly from either side and begin to build an urban strategy on the more solid foundations of a Calvinist world and life view. The Biblical Gospel is far larger than either the liberal social activists or the traditional fundamentalists imagine. It is a Gospel which includes winning disciples to Christ, establishing churches, and building a Christian community with all its facets and areas of concern. The whole city, from top to bottom, must be called to repentance toward God and faith in the Lord Jesus Christ. This is the full Gospel which requires the total renewal of man and his society, and it is the only Gospel which offers any genuine hope for today's urban world' (From *Discipling the City*, 1979, p.278).

Such was no doubt the vision of Dr. J.A. Mackay in founding the Colegio San Andres in Lima, Peru.

Such, then were at least some of the motives which characterised our Free Church foreign missions immediately following the Disruption – the consciousness of carrying out Christ's great Commission in the conviction that God is Sovereign over all the earth and all the peoples and that the Christian is called to bring this message to the whole world. Missionaries worked in the confidence that the kingdom of Christ would indeed grow amongst all the nations.

THE CHRISTIAN WITNESS TO THE JEWS

We have mentioned that the Church in Scotland had begun to take seriously its own Confessional statements which urged the propagation of the Gospel to those who are without, especially to the Jews.

The cause of the Christian witness to the Jews as far as our Church was concerned was started in a serious way as a result of the well-known 'Mission of Enquiry to the Jews' undertaken by Rev. R.M. McCheyne, Rev. Dr. Andrew Bonar, Rev. Dr. Black and Rev. Dr. Keith, an enquiry undertaken at the behest of the Church of Scotland in 1839. As a result of this five missionaries were appointed to the great work of Jewish evangelism and commenced this work in Eastern Europe – in Moldavia, Constantinople and Budapest, initially meeting with great success. All of these missionaries were received into the Free Church in 1843.

The Christian evangelisation of the Jews was based upon strong theological foundations – the same great post-millenarian 'hope' that inspired the mission to the Gentiles. That 'hope' also held that in 'the prolific womb of the future' there was to be a turning of Israel to the Lord Jesus Christ and with this a great blessing from God to the whole world. A neglect of taking the Gospel to the Jew was seen by many of the best spiritual people in the Church as tantamount to disobedience to Christ and laying the Church open to Christ's wrath. We should cherish as a precious privilege the opportunity of taking Christ's Gospel of salvation to those of whom he was a member according to the flesh.

THE FREE CHURCH'S MISSIONS AT THE CLOSE OF THE 19TH CENTURY

The Free Church of the 1890s was a very different church from that of the 1840s. To be sure the Church's missions had developed very greatly and were now operating in seven distinct areas, viz. India, Arabia (Aden etc.), the New Hebrides, Syria (Lebanon), the Eastern Cape of South Africa, Natal, and in what is now Malawi. In addition there was the Jewish work and the great work amongst the colonial settlers.

But there was a drift in the theological position of the Church and the great warriors of the Disruption era had gone. The deep springs of evangelical, Puritan faith seemed no longer to satisfy the Church's leaders and entrance was given to a destructive modernism in theology that boded ill for the younger churches also.

When the majority of the Free Church went into the Union with the United Presbyterian Church in 1900 all of the missionary staff of the Church went too and with them they took all the missionary institutions and properties that had formerly come under the name of the Free Church of Scotland.

For the remnant Free Church that survived this crisis, the loss of all its missionary work was tragic. Of course the work continued under the new Church's name but it is true to say that by the turn of the century much of the old Reformed evangelicalism had gone, and this was to be reflected in the theological positions of the younger churches too.

THE POST-1900 FREE CHURCH AND ITS MISSIONS

Although the Free Church lost all its missionaries and all its mission work in 1900, yet the Church did not lose its missionary vision – '... the Free Church of today is imbued with the same missionary spirit which formed so conspicuous a feature of her earlier activities ... After the separation of 1900 the Free Church was ... ready to do all that in them lay to discharge this supreme function of a Christian Church' (Stewart & Cameron, *Free Church of Scotland 1843–1910*, pp.399–400).

While one must grieve at the great loss suffered by the Free Church through the loss of 'her' mission fields, one has also to be grateful to God for the missionary vision left within the Church. The odds against the Church surviving in Scotland were, in human terms, small indeed. It was not the material loss which had the greatest effect upon the Church's morale, it was the bitterness and misrepresentation. The continuing Free Church was not given long to live. A similar disinformation campaign seems to have been employed on at least some of the mission fields.

But be that as it may, the Free Church followed its vision and set about establishing a missionary work which eventually re-established its presence in both India and Southern Africa and introduced it to Peru. It continued to bear a Christian witness to the Jews. In terms of manpower and resources the work was now small indeed. Yet relative to the size of the continuing Free Church it compared favourably with even the best days of its former endeavours. It was a continuing lament of Dr. Alex. Duff that so few offered themselves for missionary service and how some members only contributed 'the fifty-second part of a farthing weekly, for the conversion of the world!' (Address to the Free Church Assembly 1872).

As the continuing Free Church developed its (new) missionary work in its three main spheres of labour it incorporated in that work what it had always done well in the past – education and medical work. In the changing circumstances which developed, the medical work became no longer possible under the Church's banner, and, as far as the African field is concerned, church schools were all incorporated into the national education system. The work continues to develop the indigenous churches but in all of our missionary areas we find a lack of national pastors. The Lord must surely be asking us to look seriously at this.

FACING THE FUTURE

The supreme function of the Church remains the same: the Great Commission of Christ – that the Church must 'go and make disciples of all men . . .' (Matthew 28:19). As we have looked back to see what motivated our Church's missionary effort in the past we must formulate definite goals for our continuing effort to fulfil our commission. 'The motive in founding a mission is decisive to its ultimate success' (Stewart of Lovedale).

The theological motives remain – we are a Church committed unreservedly to the great Reformed and Puritan traditions with the injection of that deep evangelical warmth that is a feature of Scottish theology, rescuing it from the dangers of a cold scholasticism.

The methodology of fulfilling our missionary vision has to be thoroughly Biblical also and applied in ways in which we can be of the greatest service in the conditions prevailing in those areas where we mission today.

For example, in South Africa church schools were taken over by the Government many years ago, but a strong Christian emphasis remained. In the emerging 'new South Africa' there are strong indications that the state will be a 'secular' state with no state recognition of Christianity and the education system will be directly affected. There may well come a definite need for the Church to consider setting up (private) church schools again.

Dr. J.A. Mackay states: 'I take it that we are not . . . to challenge the validity of educational effort as a legitimate aspect of missionary activity, nor yet to question the utility of missionary institutions of an educational character'. He goes on to say that the three great aims of such activity should be: 1. to produce a supreme Christian impression; 2. to educate the whole Christian community ('. . . the education of no member of the Christian community should be left to institutions not controlled by Christian ideals and permeated by a Christian spirit'); 3. the preparation of Christian national leaders (*Vision of the Kingdom*, pp.85–88).

The provision of a church-related medical service may also come to be a possibility.

Theological Education

In all our missionary areas there is a pressing need for theological education to be given to our younger churches. Is it a coincidence that at this very time God has supplied us in the Free Church with an abundance (a surplus?) of well-qualified younger ministers who could lay their gifts at the roots of the younger churches to help develop them in the 'faith once delivered to the saints'?

In the past the Free Church showed its vitality in meeting the great spiritual and social needs of Scotland and areas of the world where God opened up opportunities for mission. The great changes happening throughout almost every region on earth today are staggering. In the midst of these changes much of our traditional mission work in all our overseas fields has been deeply affected. Opportunities once enjoyed are now closed to us. Yet the Lord's Great Commission remains and we must still 'go into all the earth to preach the Gospel'. Some opportunities have passed but there are new fields opening up, new areas of great gospel opportunity being given to us. Are there men and women among us to take the command of Christ seriously?

What Kinds of Missionary Opportunity do we Have?

It may well be that our Church will not be called upon to plant young churches in previously un-Christianised areas (such as was done initially, eg in South Africa and Peru). Today we may well simply act as facilitators to help young or struggling churches to establish themselves in areas where they are already witnessing.

Help can be given with Youth Development Programmes (such as the EEFC camps programme), with Christian Literature production and Distance Education Programmes (such as come from Dumisani Bible School in S. Africa). David Barrett wrote in 1968, 'It is impossible to overestimate the importance of the Bible in African Society . . .' (*Schism and Renewal in Africa*, p.127). At the same time he notes the tragic splintering of the church in Africa when the people received the Bible in the vernacular – because this was not accompanied by an effective programme of educative literature to help people rightly to interpret and apply the Scriptures.

May the church not, in co-operation with younger or struggling churches, implement theological education to train men for the ministry of those churches who do not have the means to do this themselves?

These are but a few of many examples which can be quoted – and in which our Church may well have the resources to help.

Of course we continue to have a responsibility for ensuring the viability of the projects we have already initiated and we must train the leaders of 'our' younger churches in the doctrines of the faith, to work for a sympathetic transfer of leadership and to encourage an ongoing co-operation in the Lord's work. For this reason both Peru and South Africa still cry out for missionary helpers. Who will go?

The opening up of Eastern Europe, our awareness of the spiritual need within the European Community, and the many talented Christian young men and women in our Church should surely lead us to think that God has given us work to do, and people to do it.

When the Disruption Church took up its missionary responsibility it was motivated above all by its awareness of God's sovereignty over all the nations of the earth. This Sovereign Lord still challenges us, indeed commands us, to 'go and make disciples of all the nations'. May the present generation of Free Church members be no less zealous in obeying that command than were their Disruption forefathers. And may we be no less optimistic than they were either as we look for that day when 'the crown of all the earth' will adorn the head of our Saviour Jesus Christ.

6

Outlook on the World: The Ecumenical Interest

RONALD MACKENZIE

ECUMENISM: WHAT IS IT?

'I believe in the holy catholic church.' In common with Christian churches everywhere we adhere to this ancient credal statement of the so-called Apostles' Creed. While denying Rome's exclusive claim to be identified with that one 'holy catholic church' we nevertheless do believe in the holiness, catholicity and unity of the Church of Jesus Christ. Perhaps we should clarify what we mean by holiness, catholicity and unity.

By holiness we understand that separation of the Church from the unbelieving world with its ungodly lifestyle and her submission to the headship of Christ and to the authority of His inerrant Word. The Church or body of believers is, in New Testament language, 'a chosen generation, a royal priesthood, an holy nation, a purchased people' (I Peter 2:9).

By catholicity we mean that the Church is not confined to any one nation or place but is universally found wherever 'one Lord, one faith and one baptism' are embraced. Wherever Christ's lordship over the whole of life, belief in the Holy Scriptures as the rule of faith and baptism as an outward sign and seal of the covenant of grace and badge of discipleship is acknowledged, there the Church is found.

The unity of the Church derives essentially from the union of each member with Christ the Head. This union being by faith, implies the obedience of faith in regard to all the fundamental doctrines revealed in Scripture – eg the Deity of our Lord and His actual bodily resurrection from the dead. Rejection of such doctrines is disruptive of unity in the faith. Radical unbelief is schismatic.

Insistence on the fact that unity in Christ implies unity as regards the content of the faith publicly avowed, determines the Free Church concept of ecumenism. It is due to the obvious and deep divergence in regard to what constitutes Christianity that our Church is not identified with the World Council of Churches or with the organisation known as Action of Churches Together in Scotland (ACTS). While remaining aloof from these bodies we deny that this is sectarian. There is true and false ecumenism. The brand which tolerates a wide range of religious opinions not necessarily founded on the teaching of the Bible is obviously false.

If the Church of Christ is the 'pillar and ground of the truth' she cannot speak with two voices. She cannot speak both truth and error. She cannot proclaim both the Apostolic Gospel and 'another, which is not the gospel'.

The goal of true ecumenism as understood by the Free Church therefore, is cooperation and, where possible, union with those who adopt the doctrines articulated in the Westminster Confession and other Reformed symbols such as the Heidelberg Catechism, the Belgic Confession and the Canons of Dort. We do, in fact, attempt to establish fraternal relations with those who faithfully adhere to these standards – even though organisational union may be impossible.

SCHISM OR SEPARATION?

The Shorter Oxford Dictionary defines schism as 'A breach of the unity of the visible Church, the division of the Church, or of some portion of it into separate and mutually hostile organisations; the condition of being so divided'. It is condemned as sin in Scripture. Apostolic warnings were given against it: '... mark them which cause *divisions* and offences contrary to the doctrine ye have learned; and avoid them' (Rom. 16:17), 'For ye are yet carnal: for whereas there is among you envying and strife and *divisions* are ye not carnal and walk as men?' (I. Cor. 3:3). In Ephesians chapter 3, Paul refers to 'the unity of the Spirit' and the 'unity of the faith and of the knowledge of the Son of God'. Christian believers were to love as brethren, to seek peace and maintain unity as members of Christ. To breach this unity was schism.

We must however distinguish between the sin of schism and separation in the interests of truth. The distinction has been well expressed by J.H. Thornwell: 'Schism always implies a breach of charity; it breaks the bond, not of external, but of internal union, and is generally grounded in error of doctrine, irregularity of government, or rebellion against lawful discipline. Churches, however, may be distinct and separate, and yet perfectly at one in every principle of faith and order' (J.H. Thornwell: 'Reasons for Separate Organisation': *Works*, Vol. 4, p.441). Although separate, the Free Church of Scotland has never been schismatic. Nor can the 1843 Disruption or her refusal to enter the 1900 Union be regarded as schismatic. There was separation from Erastianism and the Courts of an erastian Church but not from the principles, doctrine or practice of the Church of Scotland. She remained the true Church of Scotland Free and Protesting.

Fragmentation of the visible Church is something grievous to a genuine Christian. Only the enemies of the Cause of our Redeemer will rejoice over needless separations accompanied with bitterness and rancour.

Separation, however, may be necessary; loyalty to the truth, loyalty to the Redeemer Himself, may require it. Schism it *may* be called, but if so, it is the only justifiable kind of schism permissible. As James Bannerman expresses it: 'That a particular Church may itself apostatise from the faith, or be guilty of imposing upon its members terms of communion, to comply with which would be sin, there cannot be a doubt that in such a case a separation becomes a duty to be discharged and not an offence to be avoided. But in separating in such circumstances from the Church, the schism lies not with the parties who separate, but with the Church that compels and causes the separation' (Bannerman: *The Church of Christ*, Vol. 1, p.48).

UNITY OR UNIFORMITY?

Our ecumenical perspective extends beyond our material boundaries and embraces all like-minded Reformed brethren throughout the world who love the Truth as it is in Jesus. On the international scene, national, cultural and linguistic differences necessitate separate Reformed Evangelical Churches.

That such uniformity is necessary and agreeable to the pattern of the apostolic church appears plain from the different nationalities that composed the different churches, in Rome, Corinth, Ephesus, Galatia and elsewhere. No doubt the widespread influence of Greek culture and use of the Latin and Greek languages within the context of the Roman Empire with its provincial administration and channels of communication contributed to a greater sense of cohesion and measure of uniformity in the Church than is possible today. But changes are taking place with the liberation of eastern Europe from communist control and the process of EEC unification. Our aim at present should be unity within the context of a multiformity of national churches.

On the domestic scene, however, uniformity is highly desirable provided there is no sacrifice of Scriptural principle in worship or practice.

In R.B. Kuiper's words: 'Multiformity does not obscure the unity of Christ's Church, but rather causes it to stand out the more boldly. Unity that comes to expression in uniformity may well be and usually is superficial' (R.B. Kuiper: *The Glorious Body of Christ*, p.14). This may be true but one cannot help feeling that within Reformed circles today there is a widespread complacency or indifference to the concept of outward uniformity in the Church. Whatever the reason – whether denominational pride, a spirit of sectarianism or self-righteousness, or fear of being swallowed up within a larger organisation – the fact is, that even writers such as R.B. Kuiper do not attach much weight to the idea of outward uniformity. In Kuiper's own words: 'Uniformity among Christians is not necessarily a good' [*ibid.*, p.43]. To be fair to Kuiper it must be said that his objection is not to uniformity in principle but to that uniformity or extreme unionism which finds its expression either in Roman Catholicism (claiming a monopoly of the truth), or in modernist churches which belittle doctrinal belief in the interests of WCC unity.

UNITY: VISIBLE OR INVISIBLE?

Evangelical Christians would agree that the ideal pattern of visible Church unity is that which we find in the New Testament Church. Whatever geographical, ethnic or linguistic differences separated them into localised churches, for example, 'the church *which is in Corinth*', they formed one universal or catholic Church, united, in varying degrees of faithfulness, purity and goal, in one Lord, one Faith, one Baptism.

That a unity already exists among all true believers throughout the world regardless of denomination – the unity of the Church invisible or election of grace (that is, invisible to *man* but not to God) is undeniable. They are all regenerated and indwelt by the Holy Spirit, united by Him to Christ, the Living Head of His regenerate people, adopted into the one Family of redeemed sinners; in short, they are all saved by grace through faith alone, 'worshipping God in the Spirit, rejoicing in Christ Jesus and having no confidence in the flesh'. The problem of unity does not lie here. It lies in the visible Church and its branches, in the absence or lack of visible unity or fellowship among these who profess to be the members of Christ.

The Church visible, in the words of our Confession, consists of 'all those throughout the world that profess the true religion together with their children, and is the kingdom of the Lord Jesus Christ, the house and family of God, out of which there is no ordinary possibility of salvation'. Like the Church invisible, this visible Church is also catholic or universal. Professor John Murray in his article entitled 'The Nature and Unity of the Church' criticises the sharp distinction sometimes made between the church visible and the church invisible and the tendency among Reformed brethren to escape their obligation to seek an outward unity by sheltering under the concept of the unity of the invisible church.

Referring to the term 'the body of Christ' as figuratively applied to the Church, Murray notices the 'organic' nature of the relationship as something far removed from anything else in this world – that of a body deriving all its life from Christ its Head. It is also a unit, all its members being united to the Head and to one another. In connection with the unity or oneness, Murray warns: 'we may not attempt to escape from the implication of this oneness and the obligation incident to it, by taking refuge in the notion of the invisible Church' ('The Nature and Unity of the Church', *Collected Writings*, Vol. 2, p.332). Murray has placed his finger on the problem. The widespread complacency or indifference to the idea of outward uniformity – (or, worse still, hostility) – is due to this kind of 'escapism'. However mortifying to ecclesiastical pride or self-interest, the obligation to seek a visible 'oneness' cannot be evaded.

This obligation arises not only from the apostolic injunctions warning against divisions and exhorting unity among believers but especially from the well-known words of our Lord's Prayer in John's Gospel chapter 17 verse 21 'that they *all may be one*, even as thou Father art in me and I in thee, that the world may believe that thou didst send me'. To refer these words only to the *spiritual*, or unseen unity of the invisible church, will not do. That 'the world may believe' it is by being convinced of something that is seen – something observable. An outward manifestation of that essential unity must be in view. If so, then true ecumenism or outward unity must be taken seriously.

Surely our Lord had in view the deepening of that spiritual love essential to the communion of saints, that bond of peace and unity of the Spirit which reflects the heavenly glory and origin of the Church. But, as Bishop Moule observes: 'that can only take place, in any connection with the unity of the saints where that unity is such that it is the unmistakable effect of the present Christ in His living power and where it glorifies and makes visible its holy cause by its own heavenly character of self-forgetting love' (*The High Priestly Prayer*, by H.C.G. Moule, p.170).

R.B. Kuiper and John Murray agree. 'When', says Kuiper, 'in His high priestly prayer, Christ pleaded for the spiritual unity of believers He must have had in mind also the *outward manifestation* of that unity' (*Glorious Body of Christ*, p.45). 'To maintain', says Murray, 'that unity belonging to the Church does not entail ecumenical embodiment is to deny the catholicity of the Church of Christ. If the Church is catholic, then *unity is catholic*'. Murray proceeds to note the sustained emphasis on oneness, the pattern being the transcendental oneness of the Father and the Son.

PROSPECTS FOR UNITY

It is apparent that the outward unity our Lord had in mind was *unity in the truth.* This is the only unity which we in the Free Church can seriously contemplate. Indeed we may go further and say that it is *the* unity that we should long for and earnestly pray for. As John Murray pertinently observes, this unity specifically embraces 'all those who believe on Me *through their Word*'. 'It is', he continues, 'monstrous travesty to make the prayer of Jesus the plea and warrant for the kind of affiliation represented by the World Council of Churches. Further, our Lord's words, "as thou Father art in me and I in thee" make mockery of any unity not based upon the doctrine of the Father and the Son which the apostolic witness provides' (*ibid.* p.335).

In its Report on Ecumenical Relations submitted to and adopted by the Free Church General Assembly in 1984 consideration was given to relations with those churches 'which avow and make serious endeavours to practise the faith as articulated in the historic Reformed symbols'. Pertinent questions asked were: 'Should such Churches cohabit in the same country in the use of the same language, as separate branches of the Church of Jesus Christ? Is it obedience to the will of Christ that makes them retain separate identity – or disobedience? Is their separation a righteous or sinful thing?'

From the standpoint of what we could describe as scriptural ecumenism the answers must be obvious. Such Churches have no justification for remaining separate. Nor can it be shown to be obedience to the will of Christ for such divisions to continue. Such separation, whatever the justification originally claimed for it (as for instance, the 1892 Declaratory Act, subsequently rescinded by the present Free Church in 1905) can no longer be justified. It is therefore sinful; it is schismatic. Divisiveness fosters a self-righteous censorious spirit inimical to brotherly love.

THE DENOMINATIONAL SCENE AND OUR OWN IDENTITY

Our quest for unity in the truth must take account of the denominational scene in Scotland. As a Presbyterian church our first concern must be with a fragmented Presbyterianism: Church of Scotland, Free Church, United Free, Free Presbyterian, Reformed Presbyterian, Associated Presbyterian. Only when we have addressed this question can we consider the wider field of non-presbyterian ecumenism, comprehending independents, baptists or episcopalians!

The Free Churchman who has an intelligent grasp of the underlying historical and theological reasons for her present position has no difficulty in asserting her claim to be the true, lineal historic Church of Scotland, Free and Protesting. He realises that her Claim and Protest of 1842 is as relevant today as it was then – as asserting not merely her spiritual independence but her entire submission to Christ as her only Head and to *His Word as her only rule*: her Claim being based upon Holy Scripture 'in accordance with the Word of God, the authorised and ratified standards of this Church'.

Less convinced, however, are others who have little or no interest in Free Church principles. We must, we are told, look to the future and forget the past. What really matters today is a person's personal relationship to Jesus Christ, whether or not he or she is a 'Christian' and not ecclesiastical affiliation. Consequently there should be no denominational barriers to Christian fellowship and the Lord's Table. Denominational barriers are seen as an anachronism from the past and irrelevant to the present day. Should such superficial views gain widespread acceptance it can only lead to the demise of the Free Church of Scotland. It has already led to an identity crisis.

OUR RELATIONSHIP WITH OTHER PRESBYTERIAN BODIES

Church of Scotland

This is still acclaimed as the national Church and is, of course, the largest Protestant denomination in Scotland. Inevitably this lays on other Presbyterian Churches an onus of proof as to the rightness of their continuing separation from the national Church. We must be prepared to accept this responsibility. In doing so we immediately recognise that between our two Churches there is a great theological divide.

The Theological Divide

It is not our purpose to maximise denominational differences in order to justify ecclesiastical separation but to state the facts, clearly and simply. The Formula to which Free Church office-bearers are bound by their ordination vows and to which they solemnly subscribe is radically different from that of their counterparts in the Church of Scotland. There is a fundamental difference between an unqualified and a qualified subscription to the Westminster Confession of Faith. Either we 'believe the whole doctrine contained in the Confession of Faith' or we do not. In other words, our vows are different: there remains, at present, an unbridgeable theological divide.

Any attempt to bridge this chasm would require the Church of Scotland, as an ecclesiastical body, to renounce its liberalism and neo-orthodoxy and return to an unqualified adherence to the teachings of the Westminster Confession. An alternative would be for the reformed brethren within her who wholeheartedly believe and teach these doctrines to leave their liberal denomination and seek unity with the Free Church on a basis of mutual commitment to reformed orthodoxy.

Were the Church of Scotland to return to a wholehearted acceptance of confessional teaching the dream of all who strive for true biblical ecumenism and the healing of our Presbyterian divisions would be fulfilled. Alas, it remains but a dream. For Bible-believing Christians, however, unity must mean unity in the truth and can only be found in a common acceptance of the great truths of the biblical gospel. We cannot, in all honesty and consistency, remain both true and false to such truths: true to them privately and false to them publicly, by ecclesiastical affiliation. Such is the dilemma faced by godly men who, as individuals, hold fast biblical truths and yet remain within liberal denominations.

The liberalism of the Church of Scotland is highlighted by its view of the Westminster Confession of Faith. Subscription to this is qualified by Declaratory Acts which were amplified in 1929 by certain articles. These articles rendered subscription to the Confession little short of futile.

Of the Nine Articles, Article 1 defines the faith of the Church of Scotland. It makes no mention of the inerrancy and plenary inspiration of Scripture, the Fall of man and his total depravity, the covenant of grace to redeem the elect, atonement, the new birth, justification by grace through faith alone, the perseverance of the saints and their sanctification by the Spirit, the doctrine of hell and the eternal punishment of unbelievers. It may be argued that a Church failing to confess these doctrines is a Church that denies them – at least implicitly – the protests of evangelical, Reformed men within her, notwithstanding.

Care must be taken that any fellowship on a local or parochial level is not construed as honouring any particular denomination which is unfaithful to the teachings of Scripture. Otherwise confusion will prevail. Free Church people will be deluded into thinking that the differences between themselves and the Church of Scotland are minimal and non-essential. Confusion is compounded by lack of clear conviction of what the Free Church stands for. Add to this the concern – for some, the overriding concern – to evangelise our neo-pagan society. The result is that the salvation of the lost is regarded as paramount whereas ecclesiastical differences and loyalties are of such secondary importance as to be disregarded.

It sounds plausible, but is it correct? Are we not in danger of making a false dichotomy? What, after all, *is* our message for the lost? Is it not the *whole* counsel of God, the proclamation of the 3 Rs, ruin by the Fall, redemption by Christ and regeneration by the Holy Spirit? Is it not to tell them that they are in imminent danger of perishing eternally, that sin unpardoned merits eternal punishment and that faith in the Lord Jesus Christ and repentance towards God are indispensable to man's salvation? Law and Gospel are both necessary.

But the preaching of the Gospel of saving grace requires that we bear witness against the unbelief and error of the pulpits which deny these same Gospel truths. If denominational loyalty means loyalty to Gospel truth it cannot be divorced from our message. The courageous minority of 1900 were concerned not merely with conserving the original constitutional position of the Church of Scotland Free and Protesting, but with handing down to future generations the full-orbed biblical Gospel of divine Grace enshrined in her standards. Denominational loyalty is not a matter of indifference. Our loyalty is to the Word of God and as long as the Free Church remains loyal to the Word we should be loyal to her. The Gospel of Grace is *her* message and it is the only message for the lost in Scotland and in the world.

Can we Co-operate?

The theological divide ought not to blind us to our responsibility as a Christian Church for the moral and spiritual welfare of our nation. Nor should it excuse us from co-operating with all who seek to resist the inroads of secularism and to uphold Christian standards in the media and in society. We should have practical concern for the sick, the poor, the unemployed, the disadvantaged and aged members of society. Liberalism may not be Christianity but neither is that Christianity which is not 'careful to maintain good works' (Titus 3.8).

The temptation to retreat into an introverted pietism must be resisted. As a Church which holds to the Establishment principle we may and ought to co-operate with other denominations, including the Church of Scotland, in seeking to alleviate social distress, injustices and suffering in society. We ought to emulate the practical godliness of Thomas Chalmers and Thomas Guthrie. Our social and moral problems may be more complex today but they demand our compassionate concern. Ecumenical co-operation at this level, where there is no compromise of biblical principle, is not only desirable but necessary.

There is, of course, a real danger that a Church may be sidetracked into a social gospel outlook that overlooks its great and primary task of preaching the Gospel of the grace of God. We are to remember that the unregenerate mind, whether of the man-in-the-street or the modern churchman, is *only* concerned with social needs – 'What shall we eat? or What shall we drink? Wherewithal shall we be clothed?' (Matt. 6.31). The social gospel has its own appeal to the carnal mind of man. But it cannot save a soul from hell: it has no salvation from sin.

Barriers to Co-operation

Evangelical opposition to liberalism is one thing. More subtle, and on that account, more dangerous, is the increasing influence of Rome *within* larger denominations such as the Church of Scotland. This is highlighted by the recent emergence of the new ecumenical grouping, Action of Churches Together in Scotland (ACTS) which includes the Church of Rome, The Scottish Episcopal Church and the Church of Scotland among the constituent members of its organisation.

Rome's ultimate aim is to embrace all 'Churches Together in Scotland' within her fold. If the Church militant exists to contend for 'the faith once delivered to the saints', then let us not be ashamed of our Reformed heritage but sound a loud alarm against the dangers of Romish domination of Scottish religious life. Such Romeward trends only serve to widen the theological divide.

To swim against the stream of public and ecclesiastical opinion is not easy. For the sake of truth we must be prepared to sacrifice popularity. To be branded as narrow-minded, uncharitable or schismatic is nothing new. Our fathers suffered reproach for adhering to principles dearer to them than life itself. Let us cultivate a true Christian spirit without bitterness or self righteousness. This may help to disarm ignorant prejudice and silence criticism.

Let us not forget that as a Church we have our own serious blemishes: lukewarmness and lack of holy zeal, laxity in discipline and low spirituality. Ecclesiastical pride can blind us as surely as it did the Churches at Ephesus and Laodicea which merited in each case the Lord's just reproof. Has the Free Church left her first love? Can we escape the censure of lukewarmness? Our ineffectiveness should cause us great searchings of heart. We dare not hide our own Christian infidelity under the cloak of divine sovereignty. Are there not with us, even with us, sins against the Lord our God? (II Chron. 28.10).

RELATIONSHIPS WITH SMALLER PRESBYTERIAN CHURCHES

It is when we turn to the smaller Presbyterian denominations sharing the same unqualified adherence to the Westminster Confession that we realise our own shortcomings in seeking organisational unity. Unity in the truth there may be – in theory. But in practice we have denominational fragmentation which creates its own problems – apart from the fact that for brethren not to dwell together in unity is both unscriptural and unseemly.

In the north and west Highland Region, past divisions have left a deplorable situation. Three, and in some instances four, separate Presbyterian denominations are found in small, scattered, rural communities where prior to 1893 there had been but one or in some places two (the Free Church and the few who remained in the Established Church). Now we have the Church of Scotland, many of which are former United Free Congregations (prior to 1929, and Free Church prior to 1900) having a generally conservative theological tradition, the Free Church, the Free Presbyterian Church and the Associated Presbyterian Church.

To have four such bodies worshipping separately and all claiming to possess a Reformed ministry within a total population of not more than 300 souls, of whom nearly one half are non-Church going, is surely scandalous. To our own non-Church goers, incomers and others with a tenuous ecclesiastical attachment the situation appears confusing – not to say irrational. Furthermore it inhibits and hinders evangelistic outreach in the district and weakens effective Christian witness.

In addition there is the sheer waste of resources involved in manpower and in the maintenance of buildings for worship and manses. Many of these congregations are scarcely viable or not viable at all, as self-supporting charges. Where one or at the most two could be viable, three or four cannot. The events of 1893 and 1900 had consequences for declining communities unforeseen at the time.

While we would not presume to question the sincerity of motive or strength of conviction which led our APC brethren to separate from the Free Presbyterian Church we wonder if they gave sufficient forethought to the consequences of their separation *into a separate denomination*. One thing the events of 1893 and 1900 teach us is that the greatest care should be taken against breaking the unity of the visible Church. Loyalty to the truth and a good conscience demand nothing less. Ecclesiastical pride is hard to swallow and a division having once been made, the healing of that division is notoriously difficult, even when the original causes of it are removed. The Apostolic injunction is easily forgotten: 'Let all bitterness, and wrath, and anger, and clamour, and evil speaking, be put away from you, with all malice' (Eph. 4.31).

While it is easier to analyse a problem than to provide a solution, it is obvious that a solution cannot be achieved without discussion and where there is agreement as to the rule of faith and life, discussion should be possible. Old and new misunderstandings and animosities should be overcome as all parties submit to the authority of God's Word. That the Free Church should invite other Churches such as the Free Presbyterian and the Associated Presbyterian to conversations aimed at overcoming present barriers, would at least be a beginning. Initially there may be rebuffs and refusals but with patience and persistence these may be overcome. The present divided state of Churches sincerely avowing the doctrines of the Westminster Confession and applying the health-promoting discipline of the faith, must be cause of shame and confusion. Were Knox, Melville or Rutherford alive they would, no doubt, be horrified to see the broken condition of their beloved Church of Scotland. The credibility of the Church is at stake. The ecumenism must begin at home.

CONCLUSION

Two cannot walk together except they be agreed; nor can two or more Churches. Uniformity is desirable, if for no other reason than to avoid confusion. Truth is essential. Should Churches differ on fundamental biblical teachings such as justification by grace through faith alone, or on the inerrancy and infallibility of Scripture, as applied for example, to the ordination of women ministers and elders, there can be no agreement without violating truth. To do so is the road to apostasy. Polemical writing may be out of fashion in these ecumenical days, but truth requires that its banner should be clearly displayed and that its trumpet should not give an uncertain or confusing sound.

Luther, in his defence of Gospel truth – that of a gratuitous justification through faith alone – wrote: 'Here I take for my motto, *Cedo nulli.* I will give place to none. I am and ever will be stout and stern, and will not, one inch, give place to any creature. Charity gives place, for it "suffers all things, believes all things, endures all things, but faith gives no place".' This must ever govern our own ecumenical thinking and outlook.

7

Church and School and the Care of Youth

WILLIAM M. MACKAY

In 1843 the Free Church of Scotland, amongst its many other responsibilities, recognised that of developing its educational heritage. It had inherited educational principles of great value enunciated in the scheme of education set out by the reformers of the sixteenth and seventeenth centuries.

These principles may be summarised as follows:

1. Education was to be available for the children of both the wealthy and of the poor. None was to be allowed to reject it. The education of girls was specifically mentioned.
2. The system was to apply to the whole nation, graded from elementary through to university levels.
3. In order to maintain high standards of learning schools were to be visited regularly by men of learning and discretion.
4. Advancement from year to year depended on successful completion of studies for the year.
5. Education would be provided free or at reduced cost for students of ability whose parents were unable to afford it.
6. If certain levels of attainment were not reached the student should not proceed with further schooling, but be given work-related training.
7. The purpose of education had spiritual significance and was directed not only for personal benefit, but also for the common good.

Scotland was to be an educated nation.

One of the most surprising elements of the sixteenth century plan for the reform of education was its comprehensiveness. It covered the areas of primary, secondary and tertiary education in a broad, but penetrating, sweep. There was a graded inter-relationship which reflected well on those who contributed to its development. It has served as a blueprint for later developments in Scotland, and has also been used to contribute to other educational systems, especially where there has been a presbyterian presence.

It is of significance that leading Reformers often had important connections with universities. John Knox had strong associations with St. Andrews; George Buchanan with the Universities of St. Andrews and Paris; Andrew Melville with St. Andrews, Paris, Poitiers, the Academy at Geneva, and Sedan as well as being Principal of the University of Glasgow and of the New College at St. Andrews. In the 17th century Alexander Henderson held the position of Rector of Edinburgh University and Samuel Rutherford was Principal of St. Mary's College and Rector of the University of St. Andrews at the time of his death. Their contribution to education was based on knowledge and experience.

In her book, *Education in Scotland*, Mrs. M. Mackintosh writes of Andrew Melville:

'Education and civil and religious liberty had been his passions. His combination of intellectual and practical powers did more for the advancement of University education than had been accomplished in centuries. He took the Scottish Universities out of the backwoods and made them honoured as schools of learning which compared favourably with their continental counterparts. His courage, passion, zeal and love of learning typify all that is best in the Scottish character and have undoubtedly helped to foster and preserve these attributes in modern Scotland.'

That strength at tertiary level has undoubtedly contributed positively to primary and secondary levels of education.

THE EDUCATION SCENE BEFORE THE DISRUPTION

The extraordinary material and cultural progress of Scotland since 1750 was the theme of inquiry of Alexander Christison, a master at Edinburgh High School, in his book *The General Diffusion of Knowledge One Great Cause of the Prosperity of North Britain* published in 1802. According to him, although other causes were ascribed, Scotland's progress was due to the standard of Scottish education – 'a system so remarkable in its scope, so liberal in its ideas and so universal in its application that it had become the most precious inheritance which his generation had to hand on to its successors'.

In the 1820s the financial arrangements for education in Scotland were advantageous. Education was not free, but in country districts it was supported by a tax on heritors and in the burghs provision was made from municipal funds. Children could receive elementary education for far less than cost. The law could be invoked to set up a school and to ensure that the teacher's salary would be paid.

But these were the years when the Industrial Revolution was making its impact. Cities were growing at a remarkable rate. Between 1801 and 1851 Glasgow grew from 77,000 to 345,000 inhabitants; Edinburgh and Leith from 83,000 to 194,000; Scotland from 1,625,000 to 2,896,000.

Professor Smout in *A History of the Scottish People 1560–1830* quotes from the work published in 1834 by the Reverend George Lewis of Dundee entitled 'Scotland, a half-educated nation'.

'According to Lewis about one fifth or one sixth of the population fell between the ages of six and fourteen, but only one person in twelve was actually enrolled in day schools. As far back as 1818 it had been shown that of 5,081 schools involved in elementary teaching only 942 belonged to the publicly financed national sector: 2,479 were fee-paying private schools, 212 were charity day schools and 144 were charity Sunday schools. Of the children, only 54,000 (a little more than a fifth of those being educated and perhaps a tenth of those needing education) were going to publicly financed schools; 112,000 were in private schools, 10,000 were in charity day schools and 75,000 were in Sunday schools.'

These comments would be reinforced by Thomas Chalmers' experience in St. John's parish in Glasgow between 1819 and 1823. Having set up two schools to provide education for the children of the parish, he discovered that the demand was greater than could be reasonably met. He set in train the process by which another two schools were built and provided with teachers. The education of 800 children was thus provided for.

In Scotland prior to the Disruption some rural parishes were well-served and schooling was available to the majority. This was especially true in Central and Eastern Scotland. In the larger parishes of the more mountainous and island west, schooling was not readily available to the same extent.

In the burghs, intelligent literacy had been achieved in the eighteenth century, but declined, especially in the industrial towns, in the early nineteenth.

In addition, the grammar schools, the academies and the universities provided excellent education for professional and commercial training prior to 1830.

THE DISRUPTION IMPACT

With the church's involvement in education, it was almost inevitable that parish schools would be caught up in the consequences of the Disruption. It is difficult to gauge the reaction as it affected the pupils in the schools, but there were very clear consequences for teachers in parish schools or others whose allegiance lay with the Free Church of Scotland.

Dr. Welsh, in the Report on Education submitted to the Assembly a few days after the Disruption, underlined the need for opening schools in connection with the Free Church of Scotland. 'Schools must be opened to afford a suitable sphere of occupation for parochial, and still more for private teachers of schools, who are threatened with deprivation of their present office on account of their opinions upon the Church question. Such individuals should be invited instantly to give in their names to the Church, and provision should at once be made for their employment . . . They are the more deserving of attention on this account that we have not only the case of cruelly injured teachers, but still more, perhaps, of the children who are to be put into different hands.'

In Campbeltown there were nineteen teachers, male and female, in public and private schools. Whether under the jurisdiction of the Establishment, or pressurised to be under it, they were all ejected.

Mr. Carment, minister of Rosskeen, had been responsible for setting up two schools in his extensive parish, one of which was built at his expense. In 1844 the schoolmaster of that school was replaced by another on the order of the Duke of Sutherland.

Throughout Scotland, seventy-seven teachers in parish schools, sixty Assembly-school teachers and seventy-five belonging to the Society for Propagating Christian Knowledge were expelled for adhering to Free Church principles. In October 1843, the General Assembly which met in Glasgow was informed that 196 teachers in private schools had been ejected. In all, some 400 teachers had been deprived of their living and that mainly at the instigation of those who remained in the Established Church.

From that crisis arose the need to set up an Educational Scheme to provide education. Dr. Welsh had said in May 1843 that no church, aspiring to the character of national, would fulfil its mission if it was not providing for the religious training of the young from the lowest elementary school to the first institutions of science and learning.

To achieve this, funds additional to those required for ministers' stipends, church buildings and manses; additional to support for theology professors, students and a theological hall; additional to support for missionaries had to be found. In October 1843, Mr. Macdonald of Blairgowrie presented his proposal to a crowded evening session of the Assembly. He offered to raise £50,000 for building 500 schools, undertaking to travel throughout Scotland and find subscribers to the project.

The details of the scheme were set out:
'Scheme for raising £50,000 to aid in the erection of 500 schools for the Free Church of Scotland. Each school to be aided to the extent of £100'.

500	persons giving 1s to each of 500 schools yields being £25 individual contributions	£12,500
1000	persons giving 6d to each of 500 schools yields being £12.10s individual contributions	£12,500
2000	persons giving 3d to each of 500 schools yields being £6.5s individual contributions	£12,500
6000	persons giving 1d to each of 500 schools yields being £2.1s 8d individual contributions	£12,500
9500	persons giving at the above rates	£50,000

With the Assembly's blessing Mr. Macdonald ventured forth. Edinburgh subscribed £7,000, Leith £1,125, Haddington £520, St. Andrews £600, Perth £1,400, Dundee £2,700, Arbroath £1,100, Inverness £1,000, Wick £775, Paisley £1,300, Rothesay £1,000. A visit to England was not unproductive, with £500 subscribed in Manchester, £1,000 in Liverpool and £1,400 in London.

In May 1844, Mr. Macdonald was able to report that upwards of £52,000 had been subscribed. It was clear evidence that the Free Church of Scotland was fully supportive of educational enterprise.

A year later it was reported that 280 schools were already in operation. In 1847 there were 513 teachers linked with the scheme. Other schools linked with the Free Church, but not requiring support from the Committee, brought the number to 650. Returns in that year from 595 schools showed a student attendance of 44,000, not far off the numbers educated in the parish system prior to 1843.

The funds subscribed were for buildings, not for teachers' salaries. Salaries required attention and Dr. Candlish, appealing for assistance, made an important statement on the purpose and direction of Free Church interest in education.

'The more we look around us and notice the current of events, the more must we be impressed with this conviction, that if not for the sake of the Free Church itself, at least for the sake of religion and Christianity, it becomes the bounden duty of the Church to establish, not on a sectarian basis, but on broad Christian principles, a system of adequate instruction for the whole youth of Scotland who will accept it at our hands.'

In 1850 Dr. Candlish reported that there were 657 supported schools with an attendance of close to 60,000 students. Other Free Church schools, not supported directly by the Committee, provided education for another 14,000 children.

With various systems of education in existence there were problems in setting up a national system. Many leading Free Churchmen were active in seeking that this should be done. Parochial schools were closed to teachers of other denominations than the established church. Only in 1861/62 was an Act passed which loosened the connection of parochial schools with the Church of Scotland although the parish minister's influence in appointments was considerable and presbyteries retained the power of examining and superintending the schools. There was a requirement that the Scriptures and the Shorter Catechism should be taught, the State having authorised the School Boards to take the responsibility for the schools under their charge.

In 1872 the Education Act was passed and the national system of education was established. The framework of a graded system of public education was laid down, comprehending infant, elementary and higher level public schools and education was made compulsory and universal in both town and country. In 1870, the English Education Act dealt with elementary education only and the enforcement of education or not was left to the discretion of school boards.

Religious teaching was to be given at such hours that it would not interrupt or interfere with the secular instruction, and children were at liberty to withdraw from it without losing any part of the secular instruction.

In 1874 it was reported that 139 Free Church schools had been transferred to School Boards, that 282 had been discontinued (with the teachers employed elsewhere and the buildings retained by the congregations). 119 congregations indicated that they wished to carry on their schools for a time.

ALEXANDER DUFF

One of the outstanding educators of the time was Alexander Duff, a distinguished student at St. Andrews University and one who acknowledged a great debt to the life and influence of Dr. Thomas Chalmers. His influence in Scotland was great, but his impact in India was extraordinary. The extent of the impact is worth examining as a case study.

In 1843, after years of difficult labour, there was in Calcutta an educational work and associated church development that was a credit to the Church of Scotland. Far from the scene of activity in Scotland and the commotion surrounding the Disruption, Alexander Duff had established principles for working amongst the 130 million people of India and means that were effective in opening Indian thought to an intelligent understanding of Christianity. In August 1843, Duff and the four other missionaries with him in Bengal indicated their adherence to 'the Free Protesting Presbyterian Church of Scotland'.

In May 1829 Duff had been formally appointed as its first missionary by the General Assembly of the Church of Scotland. In September the missionary and his wife left Leith for London and sailed from Portsmouth on the East India Company's ship 'Lady Holland' a month later. In February of the following year, the 22 passengers and the crew were shipwrecked on Dassen Island near Cape Town in South Africa. All survived the disaster, but the cargo was lost. Duff had taken with him a library of 800 books, his journals, notes, memoranda and essays, of which 40 books were washed up in very poor state – only his Bible and Psalter surviving in reasonable condition. The second part of the voyage from South Africa to the Bay of Bengal ended in a second shipwreck in the estuary of the Hooghly. A May cyclone drove the ship aground and again the Duffs and other passengers reached safety, sheltering in the village temple until they were rescued. Help was sent from Calcutta and the passengers were conveyed to the city. The ship was later refloated and its cargo safely disembarked.

Duff had been charged to set up an educational institution, but not to do so in Calcutta. He resolved to ignore the advice in view of the advantages that he saw in Calcutta as a centre in Bengal from which to reach 500,000 people.

The difficulties of missionary work were exemplified by the lack of Christian converts after many years of labour. Those that existed were often of the lower classes and did not form a lively Christian witness. Duff chose to work amongst young people and his aim had a future as well as present purpose.

'While you engage in directly separating as many precious atoms from the mass as the stubborn resistance to ordinary appliances can admit, we shall, with the blessing of God, devote our time and strength to the preparing of a mine, and the setting of a train which shall one day explode and tear up the whole from its lowest depths.' Education, saturated with the teaching of the Scriptures, was the means to be used in bringing change. While religious instruction was of special significance, he aimed to teach every branch of useful knowledge – elementary forms at first, advancing to the highest levels of study in history, literature, logic, mental and moral philosophy, mathematics, biology, physics and other sciences. These aims were very different from those of other Christian educational institutions.

After consulting with a wise Indian adviser, Duff resolved not to teach in Bengali, Persian, Arabic or Sanskrit but to use English as the medium of teaching. This meant that students using these other languages were all learning English on an equal basis, were taught the Scriptures in English, were introduced to English literature – much of which was permeated with the spirit of Christianity – and studied the sciences in English, freed from the focus of the ideas that permeate Hindu thought.

Duff, with the assistance of a young untrained Eurasian, spent six hours a day teaching 300 Bengali youths the English alphabet. His evenings were spent preparing a series of graduated school-books called 'Instructors'. The first books dealt with interesting everyday subjects, the second with Biblical themes, especially those which were historical.

Word study was a key to discussion of the properties and uses of objects, drawing on information known to the boys and stimulating their powers of observation. The boys were encouraged to think. Their delight in gaining understanding was infectious and the school acquired a very favourable reputation in the community. His pedagogical style was in very marked contrast to the mechanical and monotonous style of teaching prevalent in India.

Within the first year the size of the school was expanded, as also its scope, in that no student was allowed to begin to learn English until he could read with ease in Bengali. These students were enriched with vocabulary and spiritual ideas derived from English literature. Alexander Duff was able to carry forward his own studies in Bengali in friendly rivalry with his students.

Since Duff's approach had been rejected out of hand by the European community, he tested the results of his first year's work through a publicly-announced examination of his students in the Freemasons' Hall. He invited an Anglican Archdeacon to preside. The boys responded with such effect that reports in the three daily English newspapers of Calcutta were totally favourable to the new venture.

In the second year hundreds of students had to be turned away because of lack of space. Saturdays were set aside for European visitors to view the school since they came in such numbers during the week as to interrupt classes. Visitors from all parts of India came to review what was being accomplished and returned home to establish educational centres on the same principles.

Duff also concerned himself with the education of girls, supported those who were involved in it and encouraged the younger generation to consider the importance of the education of women and girls.

After 3 years of labour the work of the school was fully recognised.

In correspondence, Dr. Duff wrote, 'The school continues greatly to flourish. You may form some notion of what has been done, when I state that the highest class read and understand any English book with the greatest ease; write and speak English with tolerable fluency; have finished a course of Geography and Ancient History; have studied the greater part of the New Testament and portions of the Old; have mastered the evidence from prophecy and miracles; have, in addition, gone through the common rules of Algebra, three books of Euclid, Plane Geometry and logarithms. And I venture to say that, on all these subjects, the youths that compose the first class would stand no unequal comparison with youths of the same standing in any seminary in Scotland'.

Work of a similar sort was set up in Bombay and Madras.

After the Disruption, preliminary letters from Dr. Brunton of the Church of Scotland and Dr. Charles Brown of the Free Church of Scotland reached the missionaries in India declaring that each church would continue Foreign and Jewish Missions. In contrast to the East India Company's Presbyterian chaplains, all fourteen missionaries to India gave their support to the Free Church of Scotland. They well understood that they might forfeit the College provided for them, with its library, its apparatus and other furnishings. Morally and in equity these were the fruit of personal legacies and gifts made to Dr. Duff. The honourable solution would have been to make these available for the missionaries of the Free Church of Scotland to continue their work and allow for the purchase of these buildings from the Established Church in as far as that was deemed necessary.

The committee of the Established Church rejected their approach. The work, however, had to continue and search was made for new premises in the vacation of 1843–1844. 'From all sides, Hindus as well as Christian, Anglican and Congregationalist as well as Presbyterian, in America no less than in Asia and Europe, came expressions of indignant sympathy'. By early 1844 £3,400 had been received as spontaneous gifts.

The second College having been organised Dr. Duff set about establishing branch schools in Baranuggui, Bansberia, Chinsurah, and Mahanad. Culna was retained.

Some ten years later Dr. Duff was invited to answer a question posed by Lord Stanley of Alderley.

> 'Will you state what you would propose the Government should do towards the further improvement and extension of education in India'.

Duff responded by recommending:

1. The gradual abolition of oriental colleges for the educational training of natives, liberating funds for the purposes of sound and healthful education
2. The relinquishing of pecuniary control over primary or elementary education by the Government, thus achieving considerable saving
3. That lectureships on high professional subjects such as law and civil engineering should be established on a free and unrestricted basis allowing attendance of qualified students from all other institutions and that, in Calcutta, a university might be established on the general model of London University, with a sufficient number of faculties in such a way as to stimulate and foster studies in Government and non-Government institutions

4. The use of the Bible as a class-book in English classes in Government institutions, under the express and positive proviso that attendance on any class, at the hour when it was taught, should be left entirely optional
5. The Government ought to extend its aid to all other institutions where a sound general education is communicated

These ideas formed the basis of the Educational Despatch of 9th July, 1854 signed by 10 directors of the East India Company and sent out to the Marquis of Dalhousie.

The College continued to grow. New buildings were provided and the school roll reached about 1,200, the students receiving instruction in literature, science and the Christian religion.

Duff was nominated by the Governor General to be one of those who drew up the constitution for Calcutta University. For the first six years of its history, Dr. Duff led the senate. Of his leadership Dr. Banerjea wrote, 'To his gigantic mind the successive Vice-Chancellors paid due deference, and he was the virtual governor of the University. The curriculum he promoted for the university was broad in its extent. Against the trend of the times, Dr. Duff insisted on education in the physical sciences and urged the establishment of a professorship of physical sciences for the University.'

Sir Charles Trevelyan strongly recommended that Dr. Duff be appointed Vice-Chancellor of the University. In a letter to him he stated, 'It is yours by right, because you have borne without rest or refreshment the burden and heat of the long day, which I hope is not yet near its close'. However, at the age of 57, it became obvious that the ill-health that had limited his activities from time to time required him to return to Britain.

Some fifty years on, the work begun by Alexander Duff had had extraordinary impact in the educational sphere. The two primary schools at Calcutta and Bombay had grown to 210 colleges and schools in which more than 15,000 boys and girls received daily instruction in the scriptures.

English had become the common language of hundreds of thousands of Indian students, crossing the barrier of local languages and dialects.

Communities were based on families which had benefited from the Christian influences which permeated them and Indians were providing support and assistance to their own people.

TEACHER TRAINING

The training of teachers was an issue that came to be dealt with in the early years after the Disruption. A Glasgow cotton-spinner, David Stow, came under the influence of Rev. Thomas Chalmers and, while working in a Sabbath School, saw the need for teachers to undergo training.

In 1817 he opened the Infants' Model School and from that, in 1836, came the founding in Glasgow of the first Normal (Training) College in Great Britain. When the building was completed, a debt of £11,000 remained to the charge of the Glasgow Educational Society. The Government gave assistance through a grant of £5,000 on condition that it be made over to the Established Church.

In 1843 all but one of the directors of the Society joined the Free Church of Scotland, as had all the tutors, but tutors and students of the College were obliged to move to new premises because of the link with the Church of Scotland. In August 1845 new premises were opened at a cost of £10,000 and over the following fifty years 1,716 men and 2,227 women were trained there.

In Edinburgh the process of teacher training was slower in developing. It was at first linked with a sessional school of the Tron Parish. By 1842 there was a specific building, constructed with Government assistance, to carry on the work. At the Disruption, the Rector of the College, Mr. Thomas Oliphant, and his staff joined the Free Church of Scotland. Temporary premises were found for them in Rose Street, but, in 1847, Moray House in the Canongate was acquired as the centre for the training of teachers. In the 30 years from 1863 some 2,530 teachers were trained there, using also the services of the Normal School.

In Aberdeen, training facilities were not established by the Free Church of Scotland until 1875. After some years, a building was provided for this specific purpose. At first only women were trained, but later men were also received. By the early 1890s, 565 teachers had been trained.

David Stow's influence is recognised as crucial in the development of teacher training and his book *The Training System* contains very pertinent comments on education.

'Education consists not in the mere amount of knowledge communicated, but in the due exercise of all the faculties whereby the pupil acquires the power of educating himself. It is a mould for the formation of character', and

'We ought to place the young under the most accomplished masters . . . "Learn early, learn well".'

His initiatives ensured that the Free Church of Scotland had an excellent attitude toward teacher training.

THE CARE OF YOUTH

Sabbath Schools

Another of the aspects of the work of the church at the Disruption was to provide Biblical instruction to the children of its own families and of others in the neighbourhood of the churches. In the General Assembly of 1843 Dr. Welsh said, 'A very general feeling seems to prevail that, under the new arrangements, the Sabbath School should be recognised as one of the stated congregational means of grace in connection with the Church'. He also reported that those who taught such classes had come out at the Disruption and joined the Free Church of Scotland.

A sub-committee of the Education Committee cared for the Sabbath School Scheme. Its report in 1845 indicated that 916 schools had been established with 4,248 teachers and 50,472 students. By 1850 there were 1,180 schools with 6,714 teachers and 75,290 children; for 1852 there were 9,122 teachers and 103,945 children and by 1893 there were 18,946 teachers with 222,035 in schools and classes.

From the early years of this activity a Children's Missionary Record had been published. By 1883 there was a circulation of 80,000 and £5,009 had been collected for missionary purposes. In 1893, £6,275 was contributed.

The impact of Christian teaching through congregational and mission sabbath schools was obviously of great significance.

In 1872, steps were taken to provide for those who had passed through the various classes of a sabbath school. During succeeding years, lectures, literary associations and advanced classes were arranged and activities promoting denominational loyalty were encouraged. Plans were made for a series of Handbooks to be published by T. & T. Clark.

In 1878, Dr. Alexander Whyte brought before the church the 'Welfare of Youth' scheme. It prescribed subjects for study with text books attached; set common examination papers for all competitors; and offered prizes in money or books and certificates. The names of those awarded prizes were to be read out in the General Assembly.

In its first year of implementation, 18,000 young people were known to be studying one or other of the subjects prescribed. 1,400 participated in the common examinations. By 1893 the numbers of those taking part had more than doubled.

In 1885, the Assembly approved a proposal to establish a Free Church of Scotland Guild. Its aims were to combine and develop existing agencies in connection with the youth of the Church; to promote the formation of new agencies; through organisations to give opportunity for concrete action; and generally to further the religious, intellectual and social wellbeing of the youth of the Church. A scheme of 'Daily Bible Readings' was also issued as part of the work of the Guild.

By 1893, there were 361 affiliated societies. A monthly magazine, 'Youth', was established, including essays, short stories, poems and even works of art. From all parts of the country, even the remotest, papers were contributed showing wide reading, reflection and very considerable imaginative and literary powers.

The Ladies Association

In 1850 Dr. Mackintosh Mackay of Dunoon put forward a scheme for educational and religious improvement in the remoter parts of the Highlands and Islands. The idea was that schools be set up in areas destitute of educational provision and that students be given training to help them meet the needs of the people there.

Dr. Mackay appealed to the ladies of Scotland for assistance with the project, especially to those of Edinburgh and Glasgow. In April 1851, with support from the Edinburgh Ladies' Association, five schools were opened in Harris.

The island of Eriskay was visited by a representative of the Glasgow Ladies' Association and it was found that in a population of 300 only three could read. There was only one complete copy of the Scriptures on the island.

In the Hebrides as a whole, some twenty years later, only 2.4% of the population could sign their names.

The students who taught in the schools studied theology during the winter months, taking the regular classes in studying for the ministry. From April onwards they taught during summer and autumn, training a promising pupil to carry on the work in their absence.

The course of instruction varied with the locality. Gaelic was the language of the school, especially in teaching the Bible and Catechism. English was also included and instruction in Latin, Greek and Mathematics if the students were able for it.

The poverty of the people made it impossible to charge fees, and clothing had to be provided for some of the children if they were to attend school.

The schools were often missionary schools and became centres for religious life. The students visited those who were ill and held meetings for young and old.

The Edinburgh Association held schools at 116 stations and gave assistance at 17 others. Glasgow, to a lesser extent, also provided valuable support.

The funds for these projects were raised, without grants from the Church, by the ladies through private subscriptions and legacies. Over a period of 30 years over £44,648 was raised and used to supply the needs of deprived areas.

THEN AND NOW

The concern of the Free Church of Scotland for education in the period after the Disruption followed the pattern initiated prior to 1843. The seed of the educational movement had been sown by Thomas Chalmers and others and its growth after 1843 reflected the strength of the base that had been established before that date.

The focus of the movement was not directed specifically at Primary or Secondary education, but at ensuring that across the spectrum there was good and improving provision both in day and sabbath schools. To that end teacher training was given an impetus that remains to this day in the facilities that exist for this purpose, although under different governance. Nor were men of the Disruption absent from the Universities, where Sir David Brewster, as Principal of St. Andrews and later Edinburgh, played a notable part and Dr. Alexander Duff was so deeply involved in the founding of the University of Calcutta.

Breadth of vision in providing for education on a national scale, not simply on a denominational basis, was yet another facet of the action of the Disruption Church. And not only on a national scale. Miss Mure of Warriston had a vision of educational opportunity in Melbourne, Australia and provided £200 for two years so that an experienced educator would have a salary suited to his position and responsibility in founding an academy there. Scotch College, as it is now, has provided generations of leaders to Australia. As with Scotch College, so with many other educational institutions around the world, the missionary international focus of the Church's vision complemented its response to need in Scotland.

Education, for the members of the Disruption Church, had a driving principle which was the spiritual kingship of Christ over His people. Alexander Duff, in an address to the General Assembly in 1844, recommended the founding of a new professorship in the Free Church of Scotland Divinity College, that of missions and education. He said, 'I have purposely conjoined "missions and education", as both united would comprehend a discussion of the best modes of imparting all useful knowledge, human and divine, to old and young, of all classes and of all climes, founded on the constitution of the human mind, history and experience, and, above all, the Word of God'. A wise and discerning vision.

For the future, those who, as Christians within the historic Presbyterian tradition, wish to contribute positively to education in Scotland have pathways signalled by the principles enunciated in the past, such as

> the availability of quality education to all, recognising the varying levels of aptitude of individual students and the need to care precisely for each one;
> a graded system which flows from primary, through secondary to tertiary education with strength and competence in early literacy and numeracy programmes; with breadth and intellectual challenge in secondary programmes and pathways at appropriate levels into technical, business and vocational activities; and a range of tertiary studies that includes rigorous investigation in the arts, sciences and other branches of knowledge;
> quality in education at all levels maintained by careful administration and monitored on a regular basis by those who have the understanding and competence to do so;
> progress from stage to stage of education to depend on attainment of skills and knowledge at a level that builds in the likelihood of further advance and confident accomplishment;
> education seen to be valued and to be worthy of support by the families who benefit from it at a level that they can afford: total support and assistance to be given where necessary;
> spiritual and moral direction based on the teaching and understanding of the Scriptures.

Such ideas are relevant to late twentieth century thought and will remain valid as we enter the twenty-first. Alexander Duff gave good advice:

'You must get the young on your side. Give me the school books and the schoolmasters of a country, and I will let any one else make not only its songs and its laws, but its literature, sciences and philosophy too! . . . Already it is the boast of our country that it has replenished the service of our sovereign with warriors and statesmen; supplied every civilised nation with men accomplished in learned professions; filled the exchanges of every metropolis in the globe with enterprising capitalists; sent intrepid adventurers to explore the most barbarous and inhospitable climes. But let us, through the medium of works for the young, and especially of school books universally adopted, only saturate the juvenile mind of the nation with evangelistic principles, duties and motives, and our country may be destined to earn yet greater and more lasting fame. Our parochial schools may become the rudiment nurseries, and our colleges, and especially our divinity halls, the finishing gymnasia of a race of men who shall aim at earning higher trophies than flags and standards rolled in blood – nobler badges than mimic stars of glittering dust; – a race of men, on whom shall fall the mantle of the Eliots and the Brainerds of the West, and the Martyns and Careys of the East.'

8

The Headship of Christ in a Pluralist Society

CLEMENT GRAHAM

The Disruption controversy was about 'the crown rights of Christ'. That Christ is Head and Lord of the Church and has appointed a structure of government and godly administration within it was the basic principle for which the 'Disruption worthies' contended. No external power had the right to interfere in the Church's internal arrangements: in this the Church was directly, wholly and exclusively accountable to the Lord Jesus Christ. So, when civil authorities insisted on interfering in those arrangements by demanding that ministers be admitted to parishes on their say so they had to be told quite bluntly that they were exceeding *their* authority and must desist. They refused to desist and were deemed to have breached a covenant of mutual helpfulness which had properly obtained between Church and State and so the leaders of the Free Church of Scotland denounced the broken covenant. They declared themselves willing to resume the previous friendly and helpful relationship should the broken covenant be restored.

At the heart of this generally understood covenant was acknowledgement of the supreme Kingship of Jesus Christ over all things – over Church and State. The State was recognised as an institute of God designed for the protection, well-being, good order and peace of its citizens. The State had a sovereignty delegated to it by God in terms of which its citizens were obligated to obedience in the Lord. The Church as a distinct and separate institute of God was designed as the communion of saints and the propagator of the Gospel of redemption. As together institutes of God it was obvious that the two structures were obligated to help and nurture one another without interference by either in the province of the other.

What is of interest to us in this article is that the Disruption controversy did not call in question the universal Lordship of Jesus Christ. Indeed it proceeded on the acceptance of this by both parties. What was in question was how this Lordship is differentiated as between Church and State.

In the mid-eighteenth century, Scotland – and for that matter the whole United Kingdom – could with some degree of legitimacy be called a Christian nation. This is not to assert that the total or even the majority of the population was fully committed to the service and worship of Jesus Christ. But there was a general formal recognition that the Bible is the Word of God and acceptance of the main teaching of the Bible in setting the tone of the religion and moral life of the nation. However lacking some might be in the vitality of true Christian experience most had no difficulty in designating themselves Christians. Adherents of other religions were few and mostly unobserved. Religious controversy was, for the most part, within the parameters of Christianity itself – notably as between Protestant and Roman Catholic and though this often strained tolerance up to and beyond people's limits, the issues of pluralism as we know them today were practically non-existent.

What this meant was that in Church and State there was formal recognition of the supreme and absolute sovereignty of God and this sovereignty was exercised by His Son Jesus Christ to whom all power and dominion had been committed. Civil authority was answerable to the same God as ruled in the Christian Church. The State could not with good conscience pass laws that violated Christian principles. The State was answerable to God and could properly allow only what God allowed.

Since these days the climate of opinion and belief in the country has dramatically changed. There are still vestigial remains of our Christian past discernible in the general life of the nation but no one would be foolhardy enough to describe Scotland or Britain as in any reputable sense a Christian nation. As a consequence the general concept of the State as an institution has radically changed. With the widespread acceptance of humanism and notions drawn from the theory of biological evolution the State has come to be regarded as something which has evolved in the course of history and now operates on the basis of the consensus of the population. There have, indeed, been totalitarian concepts thrust on people but as contemporary events demonstrate these have not been durable and the will of the people is regarded as the foundation on which the State rests. The American ideal of 'government of the people, by the people, for the people' is generally accepted. If there is room in this ideal for a claim of right in the name of Jesus Christ it can only be validated by the populace. At best He can only be a titular head. Like the British monarchy itself, Christ's sovereignty has become constitutional. He reigns, if at all, by the consent of the people.

The contemporary situation has been further modified by the advent into Britain of significant numbers of people from what used to be regarded as British colonies. Most of them are not Christian or indeed humanist. Many are Muslim or Hindu or Sikh and each group expects to be awarded freedom of religious practice and the right to propagate their own ancestral beliefs. Some indeed, may have a concept of the State as existing not by the consent of the people but by the will of God – but not the God who is the God and Father of our Lord and Saviour Jesus Christ. Yet their sense of divine mission may lead them to make demands and to expect concessions which cannot be reconciled with the traditional British way of life. The Christian community therefore feels the need to reflect anew on their own basic principles so that they may react to the new situation not in fear and anger, but in a way that will honour the divine Lord whom they serve. So far as the nation as a whole is concerned we face conditions which are as important and as determinative for the future of Church and State as were ever the issues faced at the Disruption. In going back to reflection on basics we have to ask – What do we mean by the Lordship of Christ? Over whom is He Lord? – over just the Church? or over the whole world? And if His sovereign sway be universal what are we to say to those who do not acknowledge Him? And how are we to react to the demands of those who claim the right to propagate teaching subversive of the sovereignty of Jesus Christ? Is pluralism consistent with the Lordship of Christ?

As Christians we derive our information about Jesus Christ from the Bible. This is the God-given revelation and record of His being and activity and it discloses the Son of God, incarnate in Jesus Christ as God's Word and Agent in creation, providence and redemption. Because the New Testament records the actual enfleshed appearance on earth, the teaching, works, sacrifice in death and the resurrection and ascension to glory of Jesus Christ we naturally draw mainly upon its testimony. But the New is seen as the continuance and fulfilment of the Old which is also the record of God concerning His Son.

There are two unique elements about Christ described in the Scriptures. One is that He is universal Lord – Ruler of the Kings of the earth, the supreme and only Governor. The other is that He is the only Saviour of mankind. There is no other. The salvation of the human race is solely His achievement. Our common perception of the Bible as pre-eminently the record of God's saving activity may draw our attention most frequently – and sometimes almost exclusively – to the second feature but it can only be rightly appreciated in the light of the first. Both are very significant for our present study.

UNIVERSAL RULE OF CHRIST

The Bible begins with 'in the beginning God' and tells the story of the creation as God's work and so establishes the fact that 'the earth is the Lord's, and everything in it, the world and all who live in it, for he founded it', and it is a fact of experience that people have a sense of accountability which appears to be ineradicable. This seed of religion in the human heart bears testimony to the God who is over all, the ultimate authority. On the whole, people have little difficulty in acknowledging that there is a God who rules. They may be puzzled and perplexed by features of His rule – so confused at times as to be brought to the verge of atheism. But still the conviction remains. There is a God and if there is a God He must be in control. (It is an interesting thing that on the very day this is written, it has been claimed in a radio broadcast that 80% of the people in Scotland believe in a God. This despite the fact that practising Christians are in a minority.)

A basic assertion of the Bible is that God reigns. But the Bible is more specific than that. It tells us who the Lord is who reigns. In the ultimate this is the triune God, Father, Son and Holy Spirit and this God is revealed to us in the Person of the Son who became incarnate as Jesus Christ. Jesus Himself made the claim, 'All authority in heaven and on earth has been given to me' as He issued the Great Commission. This was in harmony with statements made in earlier discussion with the Jewish leaders. 'The Father has entrusted all judgment to the Son ... He has given him authority to judge' (Jn. 5:22). Judgment here represents the exercise of ultimate authority as the function of the One who is described in the closing book of the Bible as 'The Ruler of the kings of the earth' (Rev. 1:5) and later as 'Lord of Lords and King of kings' (Rev. 17:14). 'These are bold claims', as Greg L. Bahnsen observes: 'They forcefully counteract the popular tendency to restrict the exalted reign of our Lord to some transcendent spiritual domain or the confines of the institutional Church. Christ is entitled to, and settles for, nothing less than immanent authority over all things, including the political potentates of this earth' (*God and Politics*, p.25).

Reference has been made to difficulties – sometimes apparently insuperable difficulties – which people encounter when they recognise that Christ is in control. There is in everyday experience so much that is chaotic, immoral, unjust. Day by day via the public media our ears are assailed by reports of violence, rape and murder and our hearts are torn by pictures of suffering – even the suffering of 'innocent' babies and children through hunger and lack of medication. The Bible itself is not ignorant of these facts that seem to put God in the dock of human judgment. It records incidents of men of God who complain to Him and even of some who almost explode with anger. The facts seem to demand some sort of theodicy.

On one point the Bible is quite clear. We will not achieve a theodicy by diminishing our concept of God or of the scope of His rule and authority. We are not relieved by having recourse to a God of goodwill who is impotent to procure the benefits of His benevolence to His subjects. That is a God who opts out – a typically human reaction in difficult situations. That is not the God revealed in Jesus Christ.

Some help may be gained from reflection on different perspectives of the rule of Christ. There is indeed just the one ultimate ruler but His operation may be seen in different ways. There is the Providential rule and there is the Messianic rule of Christ and different characteristics may be discerned in each.

When we speak of the providential rule of Christ we refer to his 'ruling and governing all his creatures and all their actions'. This may appear to charge Him with responsibility for all that is. Does 'whatever is' have divine sanction? It depends what we mean by 'divine sanction'. If we mean – does it have divine approval, the answer in many cases is a firm negative. If we mean – has it a place in some overall plan of God whose details we can't know, the answer must be positive.

God – in Christ – rules over a fallen world, a world in rebellion against Him: a world which 'lies in the wicked one'. God did not choose to destroy the world immediately upon the entry of sin. In that sense he chose to tolerate sin in the world, to restrain and contain its effects, to introduce a programme of deliverance and ultimately to purify a people to Himself. This tolerance of God one usually refers to as His common grace. In common grace God maintains a witness to Himself in the human heart and in the environment. But there is also a didactic element in the Providence of God. There are things the sinner will not learn except the hard way – the hard way that involves suffering and logical absurdity. God allows human sinful processes to work themselves out – to demonstrate their inherent vice in the infliction of suffering and privation. To a large extent this was done in the Old Testament era as part of the preparation for the coming of Christ. God allowed human processes to demonstrate their redemptive bankruptcy. The best, the noblest philosophies of men left to their own cogitation procured no deliverance. 'When the world was without strength . . . Christ died'.

The apostle Paul tells us that God let what passes for wisdom in the world demonstrate its own futility in deepening ignorance of God. Over against that futile wisdom is set God's programme of salvation which though ridiculed as folly by the wise of this world proves universally effective. This programme of salvation involving, as it does, the crucifying of the Son of God not only exposes and denounces human wickedness but demonstrates how even this is under divine control. What man did in rebellion and rejection of God, God directed to the achievement of His great act of mercy. To put the matter bluntly: if anyone could be said to have a right of complaint against God: if anyone could argue that God had abandoned just rule of the world and let it go its own way – that one was Jesus Christ, the Just One. But He knew the whole plan. He saw the end from the beginning. He knew that God meant it for good for the human race and He was willingly co-operative.

When therefore we are perplexed, perhaps even enraged, when it seems that God's rule is too tolerant of evil let us come to the Cross of the Son of God. We may not achieve complete understanding – indeed we will not – but we gain those insights which are supportive of faith. We are assured that the One who is in control knows what He is doing and has a purpose to achieve through the chaos of human events. For the One in control is the One who Himself was subjected to the pressures of human injustice and Divine dereliction. This is itself sufficient to silence our hasty judgments and encourage us to patience.

We are the more reassured when we remember that the victory of Christ over death guarantees His total and universal victory over all the powers and principalities that exist – and whose influence in human affairs occasions much of the havoc and destruction that give rise to our complaints. God has enthroned His Son and commanded the nation to 'serve Him with fear'. He makes his enemies 'a footstool for His feet'. He 'exalted Him to the highest place, and gave him a name that is above every name, that at the name of Jesus every knee should bow, in heaven and on earth and under the earth, and every tongue confess that Jesus Christ is Lord, to the Glory of God the Father'.

Such is that glory accorded to Christ in His Providential rule. It is important that we appreciate its universal scope – that there is no corner of the world where the writ of Christ as King is not authoritative and demanding of obedience. Whether people read, appreciate and obey the writ or feel insulted and offended by it does not affect its legitimacy. Recognition of this fact is determinative of our approach to followers of other religions. One is aware of voices raised within the Christian community expressive of concern that the assertion of the universal sway of Christ makes impossible dialogue with the followers of other religions and this is a point to which we shall have to return when considering the implications of pluralism in the state. But it is timely at this point to rebut and reject the disclaimers of Christ's universal reign. It is just not true to the Biblical record to declare that Christ's reign is limited to the covenant people. It is true that proclamation of the universal rule of Christ gives an aura of triumphalism to the Christian message. Of course it does. Anyone who can read the declaration, 'He must reign until he has put all his enemies under his feet' and not be aware of the thrill and exhilaration of triumphalism is just not paying attention. But Christian assurance of triumph is not an incentive to oppression nor to contempt of people committed in good faith to other religions. But it is a strong incentive to mission.

Our reflection on the Providential rule of Christ may be summed up in the words of Gary Scott Smith as follows: 'Because Jesus is Lord of the universe, the ascended King over all creation, all governments are under His authority. Ultimately all earthly powers are subject to Him; His authority transcends that of all earthly rulers. Because this is so, political authority ultimately stems from God – not from the consent of the governed. Governments must respect, honour and protect their citizens, not because they possess certain inalienable natural rights, but because the Creator of the Universe assigns moral worth and value to creatures made in His image and likeness' (*God and Politics*, p.12). It is a fact which calls for emphasis that a legitimate charter of human rights will owe its validity and legitimacy not to human consensus – a United Nations

Charter – but to the gift of God. Rights are bestowed by God, not conferred by man.

MESSIANIC RULE OF CHRIST

The other aspect of the rule of Christ is usually referred to as His Messianic rule. This is the rule He exercises within the community of His believing followers – His rule in the Church. In this His authority is no less absolute than his authority over the nations but it is overtly, formally and dynamically realised and acknowledged. His people know and acclaim Him as their King. Their obedience falls short of what is due and is vitiated by ignorance, prejudice and self-will but still obedience to the Lord of Glory is the motif of the life of each believer.

The Messianic kingdom exists specifically to advance the saving purpose of God. It brings to the world that lives in rebellion against God the message of divine reconciliation – the message of the forgiveness of sins, of the love of God. It brings the dynamic of Divine love into the very heart and being of individuals so that bound together in the love of God they may transform the life of their nation. The necessary restructuring of political systems so as to achieve justice and equity for all can only be realised as people themselves are restructured in their thinking and relationships as they respond to the love of God in Jesus Christ. Every Christian has a mandate to advance the Kingdom of God. Every Christian needs to be empowered by God Himself to know and fulfil this mandate. That, in part, is why the Lord Himself prefaced the great commission with the assurance 'All authority in heaven and on earth has been given to me' and followed it with the revelation 'Surely, I will be with you always, to the very end of the age' (Matt. 28:18,20).

The incentive which every Christian has to propagate the message and extend the borders of the Messianic kingdom stems from the second unique element in the functions of Christ to which reference has already been made. It is that not only is He the only absolute Ruler, but he is also the only Saviour of sinners. On this point the Bible is quite explicit. 'Salvation is found in no-one else, for there is no other name under heaven given to men by which we must be saved' (Acts 4:12).

This monopolistic claim of the Bible in the name of Christ is, as just remarked, a great incentive to mission, and is determinative of the view that Christians entertain of other religions which also propose ways of salvation. In view of what the Bible declares, Christians must be convinced that other religions are delusive, misleading and dangerous. God's disclosure of Himself is given supremely in Jesus Christ. God's plan of salvation has been realised in the ministry and sacrifice of Jesus Christ. God's application of the benefits of that salvation is through the message that 'God so loved the world that he gave his only begotten Son that whosoever believes in him shall not perish but have eternal life' (John 3:16). This deposit of the truth God has given to the Church – not to be sealed away as too precious to share – but to be proclaimed worldwide. This salvation is on offer to all. But inasmuch as it is the Christian community who knows about it, they are the ones who must publicise the offer.

No doubt it will be argued that this represents an unacceptably triumphalist attitude. By some strange transposition of values triumph appears to have become a bad thing – one has to apologise for being put in possession of the truth! There appears to be an equation of triumph and pride. But pride has no place in the Christian incentive to mission. There is nothing in the gospel that is to be propagated which will give a foothold to pride. There is a great deal that will vanquish pride. The Gospel's exposure of sin and demerit and its insistence upon the sheer gratuitousness of salvation strips all who understand it of pride and boastfulness. 'Where is boasting?' asks the apostle Paul, and he answers 'it is excluded on the principle of faith.'

The Christian conviction that Christ is exalted above all principality and power, and that He is the only Saviour of sinners, whilst it carries with it assurance of ultimate universal triumph does not make for boastful confrontation with others. Rather it inspires gratitude and devotion to Christ and compassion and a yearning love to those known to be deluded by other systems. The approach is not insensitive to the feelings of those devoted to their own beliefs, nor unaware of the trauma associated with discovery of the error of those beliefs. It is the approach of love.

In contrast with this is a gruesome thought articulated by Krister Stendahl. 'I have been struck by the gruesome thought that universalist claims have often led to various kinds of imperialism and crusades. The connection is very simple. If my faith is universal in its claim, then woe to those who do not see the world as I do' (*Christ's Leadership and Religious Pluralism*, Edited by G.H. Anderson and T.F. Stransky, p.15).

This implies that recognition of the universal rule of Christ must inspire a dominance attitude in his followers. Such a reaction, which no doubt has occurred to the shame of the Christian Church, is contrary to the whole spirit of the gospel and the One whose grace it proclaims. The attitude of dominance turns a blind eye to the pattern of servanthood set by Jesus Himself. As He became a servant so He taught that precedence in His kingdom would be accorded to those who excelled in lowly service. Human nature is such that we too easily suppress what appear to us to be the unattractive elements in Christian service – just as the Jews in their glorious political expectations of Messiah overlooked what had been prophesied of the suffering Servant of Jehovah. Imperialist crusades are contrary to the spirit of the Gospel and have often been occasioned by issues other than that of a desire to spread the Gospel. The medieval crusades were much more concerned about the occupancy of so-called holy places than about a desire to win people to repentance and acceptance of the truth as it is in Jesus.

'Seeing the world as I do' is not to be equated with recognising and accepting the truth which God has revealed in Scripture. The imposition of private opinion is not what is at issue but the recommendation of what God has revealed. To impose private opinion people may be tempted to use any means that may promise success. To recommend the truth of God restricts to the methodology taught by God. This does not imply the 'woe' of force and terror. But there is a 'woe' which does loom large in Christian thinking. It is the eschatological woe – the threat of final destruction which hangs over those who do not accept God's mercy in Christ. The thought of that does indeed stir up the Bible believer to propagate the gospel with urgency and zeal.

What has been asserted so far then is that Jesus Christ reigns over the whole universe, all governments and authorities being subject to His providential control. More directly and recognisably He reigns over His Church. As Providential ruler He addresses people as citizens – summoning them individually as citizens and corporately as nations and in international relationships to recognise His supremacy – to seek understanding of the principles of justice and equity which He has made known and to apply them in all the varied structures of politics and society. As Messianic King He addresses people as sinners, invites them to receive His salvation offered gratuitously, and those who do receive it He bids propagate the saving word. To this end they must be bound together in fellowship and the fellowship is organised according to His direction so as to secure for each and all 'growth in the knowledge and grace of the Lord Jesus Christ'.

In reflecting on these two aspects of the role of Christ we must perceive that they are not diverse the one from the other, nor do they exist in a state of tension. In discharging different offices we may sometimes find that the claims of one appear to conflict with the claims of the other. A school teacher may sometimes face a dilemma in connection with the competing claims of parent and teacher. It is not so with Christ. We are emphatically informed that 'God placed all things under his feet and appointed him to be head over everything for the Church, which is his body, the fullness of him who fills everything in every way' (Eph. 1:22). This means that in His universal providential rule Christ always bears in mind the interests of His Church. Whatever He allows to happen in the world has a bearing on the Messianic Kingdom. It is calculated to bring certain pressures to bear upon the Church in the light of which it will look more closely at its calling and commission and react in such a way as to procure its own reformation and edification and its greater usefulness as the overt witness of Christ in the world.

That Christ rules the nations in the interests of His Church is not an exclusively New Testament declaration. The same essential truth is highlighted in the Old Testament affirmation that, 'When the Most High gave the nations their inheritance, when He divided all mankind, He set up boundaries for the peoples according to the number of the sons of Israel . . .' (Deut. 32:8). God's universal sway focuses particular attention upon the needs and functions of the people whom He claims as His special possession.

A PLURALIST SOCIETY

In terms therefore of God's rule, pluralism is almost as old as mankind itself. Very quickly after the Fall mankind divided. That division erupted in the very first family and was essentially religious in character. Abel chose the way of obedience to God. Cain chose the way of self-will and determined that God must accept what he was pleased to offer. The difference was profound and in the view of the one resolved to be his own man it was irreconcilable – hence Cain murdered Abel. But the assertion of independence on Cain's part was futile. He still found himself under the judgment of God. He went his own way but he went under judgment.

The early chapters of Genesis show how this situation of profound difference was perpetuated. As mankind increased so the numbers of those who repudiated the Living God increased. They invented their own gods, they devised their own religions, they constructed their own moral codes which ridiculed the code of truth and equity. They menaced the few who retained the fear of God, till they were almost exterminated, and at that point God brought the world under the judgment of the Flood – destroying the ungodly and preserving the household of faith, and demonstrating dramatically how His universal authority focused on the wellbeing of His Church.

A new start was made when Noah and his family emerged from the ark. But within a short time the old pattern of division was reasserted. There were those who kept the faith and there were those who rejected it and broke up into a variety of competing ways of life. The line of the faithful was perpetuated through the patriarchs – Abraham, Isaac and Jacob until Israel became known as the people chosen for special tutelage and privilege and identified as the nation and Church of God in the Old Testament era.

There were two outstanding lessons in theology which Israel learned in this era. The first was of the uniqueness of God. There is but one God and He is One. This was early learned by each Israelite as he/she became familiar with the 'Shema Israel'. It was early learned formally, but often forgotten as the people adopted the gods of other nations and practised idolatry and drew upon themselves the scorn of the prophets. Recall Isaiah's description of the man who takes a piece of wood and uses part for fuel and 'from the rest he makes a god, his idol; he bows down to it and worships. He prays to it and says "Save me, you are my god" (44:15ff). And Jeremiah exclaimed in astonishment 'My people have changed their glory for worthless idols. Be appalled at this, O heavens, and shudder with great horror' (Jer. 2:11,12).

Our contemporary situation demonstrates that there are those who profess to belong to the Christian Church who are embarrassed by the thought of the uniqueness of God. The one God and Father of our Lord Jesus Christ is labelled a 'particularity' or at any rate belief in Him alone is so labelled. This particularity has no greater claim to universal acceptance than the particularity of the Muslim or the Hindu whose gods must be regarded as equally reputable.

The second lesson in theology which was taught to Israel was implied in the first and was that of the universal sovereignty of God.

There might be those in Israel and elsewhere who thought of Jehovah as the God of the land of Israel only. Outside the limits of the nation His writ had no validity. Eventually Israel learned the lesson of God's universal sovereignty the hard way. When scattered to different lands it was made known to them that God was still with them. Indeed before the dispersal it was announced by Jeremiah that God was to bring a distant nation against them. No doubt the nation came freely to their decision to invade in the light of economic and political factors known to them. But Jeremiah insisted that God brought it about to punish his people and in doing so He revealed that his control is over all nations. Isaiah foresaw the same pattern of events and saw how liberation would come, not through a man of Israel but through 'Cyrus, my servant'.

The two lessons taught to Israel are of permanent validity and are basic to Christian belief. The New Testament reveals the One God in the Trinity of Father, Son and Holy Spirit as the only God there is and who rules over all the nations. Government has been entrusted to Christ the Saviour and He rules over all in the interests of the Church. The point of reflecting on how this Divine universal rule operated in Old Testament times is to alert us to the fact that the universal rule of the Saviour may not always be to the comfort and ease of the Church. Indeed the very reverse may be the case. A Church complacent and at ease may not faithfully and efficiently witness to the gospel of grace in the world. Just as God brought invading forces against Israel in the past, so He may bring about political situations in the world that appear to menace the very existence of the Church. Providence can be used as a sharp rebuke as well as a mighty preserver. Christian people have the very difficult task of trying to achieve some expertise in the interpretation of Providence. In the measure in which they do achieve this it is by study of the Word and prayerful communion with the Christ who reigns. Answers to our questions don't come automatically. The course of Providence often runs dramatically opposite to our expectations. A nation bans Christian missions and forbids import of Bibles as what they choose to call proselytising. How can this help the Church? How can this demonstrate that the Christ who reigns universally does so in the interests of his Church? Is his action a judgment on the nation concerned or upon the Church which may have failed to use the opportunities of mission which it had? Is it a stimulus to the Church to deploy its resources more effectively in all the nations to which it has access? Perhaps all of these factors are significant.

The almost incredible political changes which are presently taking place in Europe highlight the need and duty of the Christian Church to interpret the signs of the times. God in His Providential rule is making nations open to Christian witness which had long been closed against it. Must not the Church respond positively and energetically to the new situation?

The essential truth upon which we have reflected then is that the earth is the Lord's, that Christ rules over the whole earth determining the course and shape of events in the interests of His Church. It means that His power and influence is immanent in all nations even though most deny His authority. Much happens that perplexes and confuses the Christian community but each believer is undergirded by the knowledge that, 'in all things God works for the good of those who love Him'. The world is full of evil, tragedy and sorrow, yet it is one world under one King. He reigns over a pluralist world and will bring it to the consummation which He has determined.

OUR CHRISTIAN DUTY

The cosmic panorama is one thing, but our task is to relate it to the more immediate scene in our own nation. No doubt there are lessons of patience and tolerance and humility to be learned from study of the overall picture but how are these to be applied in our daily contact with the diverse elements of our national life? We may be afflicted with a kind of nostalgia for the past when our nation professed to be Christian and people who came to dwell in this country had to adapt themselves as best they could to the generally accepted Christian way of life. But things are vastly different now. Among those whose ancestors were Christian are many who are humanist, agnostic, atheist and they demand the same liberty of conscience and of practice as was enjoyed by their grandparents. Along with them are a great number whose ancestral roots are in India, Pakistan and other parts of Asia and who demand the right to practice the religion of their forbears. Mosques and temples are erected in a country which once knew only Christian places of worship. What, in the name of Christ should we do in this situation? How should we relate to the new population?

What is obvious is that it is the duty of every Christian to reclaim our nation for Christ. We must, individually and collectively, exert as much pressure as we can upon the 'powers that be' to reinstate the Christian ethic as the determinant factor in all law-making. We must reflect upon the Bible's teaching as to the extent and limits of civil authority so that we shall perceive the areas where witness can most fruitfully be borne. As already noted the Disruption controversy was precisely about the scope and limits of civil authority and the topic has been more exhaustively dealt with elsewhere. All that need be repeated here is that the Christian Church has a divine right to State aid in the fulfilment of its calling, and the Church has a divine right to be heard by the State as it testifies to the authority of God over the nation. No doubt there are areas of overlapping interest. It is e.g. often said that the Church's main concern is with the first table of the decalogue and the State's with the second as that bears directly on civic duty. Put more plainly, it is argued that the Church is concerned with sin in society and the summons to repentance and to pleading for forgiveness. The State, it is said, is concerned directly with crime and the need to punish, restrain, and so advance the interests of law and order. But the line of demarcation is one that may be crossed – for many sins are so obviously destructive of human society that the State must use its authority to restrain and, if possible, extinguish them. There are e.g. sins that by their very nature debase and deprave youth and the State quite properly construes their commission as crimes. The Church must therefore in the name of Christ who is Lord encourage the State to uphold the Christian ethic.

Though some may conclude that the system of party politics which obtains in our country reduces questions of moral interest to irrelevance, Christian people should, nevertheless, ascertain the attitude of candidates for Parliament to these questions. It might be profitable to remind members of Parliament that their first duty is not to party or even to country but to the Lord who is King.

Perhaps the most sensitive issue concerns the relationship of the Christian community in the country with those who comparatively are 'incomers' and who practice their own ancestral religions. They have become citizens of the country – many now by birth in the country but are still regarded as strangers by many and their presence resented. This is not the Christian attitude. Even if it were correct to speak of them as strangers there is an Old Testament obligation that was laid on Israel not to oppress the stranger. Given in a proclamation of the greatness of God it has special relevance at this point.

'The Lord your God is God of gods and Lord of lords the great God mighty and awesome . . . He loves the alien giving him food and clothing. And you are to love those who are aliens, for you yourselves were aliens.' An attitude of resentment and hostility must therefore be strongly resisted by Christians. In any case resentment is usually rooted in fear and jealousy and it would be a strange contradiction for those who claim that their God rules the universe to be afraid or jealous of others.

What is most determinative of the attitude which Christians should adopt toward followers of other religions is the methodology of the Gospel itself. The Gospel is spread and commended not by force or threat of temporal sanctions but by the persuasiveness of love. God does not forcefully compel any of us to believe. He enlightens, persuades, beseeches and woos the sinner to repentance and acceptance of Jesus Christ. God has a nobility of character and treats nobly those whom He addresses. And we must take our cue from God's method and take such opportunities as present themselves to persuade, enlighten and convince those of other religions to accept Jesus Christ as Lord and Saviour.

Reflection on how we should meet and relate to those of other religions will convince us that our point of contact is in our common sinful humanity. We share a great deal as people and as sinners. The sense of need is common to all and should make for bonds of human understanding and sympathy that can lead to more fruitful discussion. Christian people should enter into discussion with the openness of love. Eagerness to share exciting truth is far removed from the insensitive condescension that can belittle and alienate. Discussion is not exactly the same as dialogue in its contemporary definition. Dialogue, the pundits argue, involves putting everything on the line from both sides in an attempt to sieve out what can be mutually acceptable. In discussion the Christian need not – indeed will not – abandon the absolutes of Scripture teaching. To a better understanding of the Bible he is always open but this is not equivalent to questioning the validity of its obvious teaching.

Discussion must be supported and backed up by demonstration. If the Christian Gospel is essentially about the goodwill of God to mankind, it must be communicated in a spirit of goodwill. The more helpful the Christian can be to his racially distinct neighbour, the more he helps dispel confusion and fear and the sense of being unwanted, the more successful he will be in communicating the Gospel of grace.

It would be unforgivable if Christians should ignore their Muslim or Hindu neighbours. If the Christian is duty bound to try to understand the meaning of divine Providence he must ask for what purpose Christ as universal ruler has brought so many people of different religious persuasions to the country and the most obvious answer appears to be that He has provided the Church with a new opportunity for mission. The challenge of mission must be accepted.

It is a truism that belief determines action. The Christian believes that Christ his Saviour is Lord of the universe as well as Head of His Church. This delivers him from frustration and pessimism and provides a beacon of hope no matter how grim and difficult and hostile the material prospect may be. 'Our God reigns.' He is not merely a titular being but the real, energetic controlling Ruler. Reflection upon this affords the key to contentment. Because he was so sure of this the apostle Paul could affirm, 'I have learned in every situation to be content'. And always the Christian proclaims the rule of a gracious King. His rule is no threat, but the ultimate guarantee of redress for the wrongs of the world.